Favorite
BIBLE HEROES
For Grades 1 & 2

Publisher .... Arthur L. Miley

Author.. Scoti Domeij

Managing Editor ....Jack Cavanaugh

Editorial Director .... Carol Rogers

Art Director...Deborah Birch

Production Coordinator ....Chris D. Neynaber

Illustrators ....Jo Ann Hall

Terry J. Walderhaug

Proofreader.. Heather Swindle

Copyright 2000 • Fifth Printing
Rainbow Books • P.O. Box 261129 • San Diego, CA 92196

#RB36198
ISBN 0-937282-24-3

Dedicated with thanks to my father, Billy Springfield, whose insatiable hunger for the Bible instilled in me a desire to know God's Word for myself...

And to my mother, Nancy, for teaching me the importance of obeying God's precepts...

And to my precious sons Kristoffer and Kyle, who ask the most delightful questions about God, Jesus, and the Holy Spirit.

Scoti Domeij

Introduction

A hero is someone who is brave. All of the heroes in *Favorite Bible Heroes for Grades 1 & 2* were courageous. Some were weak-kneed at times, but our loving, watchful Heavenly Father always encouraged and strengthened them to perform the task at hand.

God calls each of us to lead. It may take a heroic effort on your part to face a group of little ones each week. But you have the wonderful opportunity to reflect God's loving, patient ways to an eager and watchful audience. The crafts, games, puzzles, and activities in *Favorite Bible Heroes for Grades 1 & 2* are designed to help you do just that.

Each Bible activity contains the following:
- **BIBLE HERO** name and/or picture
- **LESSON TITLE** highlighting a particular event or Bible story
- **SCRIPTURE REFERENCE** for further reading and/or background information
- **MEMORY VERSE** to reinforce the story or lesson
- **INTRODUCTION** of the Bible hero and his or her story
- **FOR THE TEACHER** directions, materials needed, and pre-class preparation
- **ACTIVITY TITLE & PROJECT DESCRIPTION** which may be read by the children.

HINTS are interspersed throughout the book and include helpful ideas for expanding the project, making it more cost effective, or adapting it to meet the special needs of each group. Suggestions for directed conversation appear in bold type. To keep costs to a minimum, send home the reproducible NOTE TO FAMILIES, requesting their help in gathering supplies. Safety should always be a priority. Close supervision is recommended at all times.

These crafts and activities highlight various aspects of just a few of the diverse people whose stories are portrayed in the pages of the Bible. When these heroes chose to obey God's instructions, they were victorious. If they failed to heed His commands, the outcome was disastrous. Daniel understood that God would protect him and he proved to be fearlessly loyal to God. Gideon lacked self-confidence and needed a bit of reassurance to be sure he was called to lead his people to victory.

The Bible honestly reflects the feelings we all face. Yet, God gently reminds us that He is in control and that we can have victory if we trust Him and do His will. As the children learn about the lives and adventures of 13 Old and New Testament Bible Heroes, they will learn what it means to love God, make responsible choices, and obey those who genuinely care about them.

TABLE OF CONTENTS

MEMORY VERSE INDEX

REPRODUCIBLE
NOTE TO FAMILIES

For your convenience, the following page contains notes to families, requesting their help in collecting the materials necessary to complete the craft activities. Hand out these notes two or three weeks before you need the items. Specify whether items should be brought in at any time or only on a specific date. Then simply duplicate the notes, and send one home with each child.

To Families of First and Second Graders

We have some exciting activities planned for use in teaching Bible lessons this year. Some of these crafts and projects utilize ordinary household items. We'd like to ask your help in saving these items for our activities:

- powdered alum
- aluminum pie tins
- beads from old necklaces and bracelets
- cardboard tubes, 4 ½-inch
- denim or old blue jeans
- wide elastic
- fabric and felt scraps
- facial tissue or tissue paper
- flowers, silk, dried, and artificial
- old greeting cards
- small jars with screw top lids
- metallic and regular wrapping paper
- milk cartons, ½-pint size
- paper plates, dinner and dessert-size
- nails
- paper cups or clay pots
- peanuts, salted or honey roasted and chocolate-covered
- pennies, new and tarnished
- plastic 2-liter bottles
- plastic drinking straws
- plastic spray can lids
- powdered milk, nonfat
- ribbon
- rocks, small and medium
- rubber bands
- salt
- shoe boxes
- unlined 3 x 5- and 5 x 8-inch index cards
- shower curtains
- flowers, silk, dried, and artificial
- empty thread spools
- yarn

Please bring the items on _______________________________. *Thank you for your help!*

- -

To Families of First and Second Graders

We have some exciting activities planned for use in teaching Bible lessons this year. Some of these crafts and projects utilize ordinary household items. We'd like to ask your help in saving these items for our activities:

- powdered alum
- aluminum pie tins
- beads from old necklaces and bracelets
- cardboard tubes, 4 ½-inch
- denim or old blue jeans
- wide elastic
- fabric and felt scraps
- facial tissue or tissue paper
- flowers, silk, dried, and artificial
- old greeting cards
- small jars with screw top lids
- metallic and regular wrapping paper
- milk cartons, ½-pint size
- paper plates, dinner and dessert-size
- nails
- paper cups or clay pots
- peanuts, salted or honey roasted and chocolate-covered
- pennies, new and tarnished
- plastic 2-liter bottles
- plastic drinking straws
- plastic spray can lids
- powdered milk, nonfat
- ribbon
- rocks, small and medium
- rubber bands
- salt
- shoe boxes
- unlined 3 x 5- and 5 x 8-inch index cards
- shower curtains
- flowers, silk, dried, and artificial
- empty thread spools
- yarn

Please bring the items on _______________________________. *Thank you for your help!*

Joshua

Exploring the Promised Land
Numbers 13-14

Memory Verse
*Be strong and courageous. Do not be terrified;
do not be discouraged.*
Joshua 1:9 (NIV)

For the Teacher
Cut a 24-inch length of string for each child. Duplicate this page for each child. Fold an 8 ½ x 11-inch piece of paper in half for each child. Punch two holes along the fold, one inch from the top and bottom. Cut two 6 x 9-inch poster board sheets and two 9 x 12-inch sheets of wrapping paper for each child. Let the children glue wrapping paper around each poster sheet. Align paper and poster board covers and punch two holes in the covers. Say, **When you feel sad or afraid, look in your journal and remind yourself of happy times. Then, give God thanks for those times. Use the journal to draw a pleasant or funny event each day.**

Introduction
Moses led the people of Israel out of slavery in Egypt. When they came to the land that God had promised them, Moses sent twelve spies to explore the land. When they returned, ten men were afraid of the people living there. Joshua trusted God and told the people not to be afraid. But ten spies gossiped and spread a bad report. God was angry that the people believed their scary stories instead of trusting Him to protect them. God told the people who complained that they would not live in the Promised Land.

Happy Times Journal
Glue wrapping paper around the poster board sheets your teacher gives you. Hold the paper and poster board as your teacher punches holes. Pull a piece of yarn through one cover, the paper, and the other cover and then back through the other hole and tie it. Cut out the title words and glue them on the cover. Inside, draw a picture of one happy thing that happened today.

Joshua

Memory Verse

The Lord your God will be with you wherever you go.
Joshua 1:9 (NIV)

For the Teacher

Duplicate this page for each child. Provide pencils or crayons. Help the children find the path to the Promised Land. As they work, talk about times when they have been scared or lonely. Remind them that God is with them no matter where they are.

Introduction

Because the Israelites did not trust God, they had to follow Moses in the desert for forty years. When Moses died, Joshua was sad. God chose Joshua to lead His people into the land that God had promised them. Joshua was feeling lonely. But God told Joshua, "I will not fail you or leave you. Be strong and courageous. Do not be afraid. The Lord your God will be with you wherever you go."

God Is Always There Maze

Follow the maze to help Joshua lead the people into the Promised Land. Trace the correct path with a pencil or crayon. Remember that God told Joshua not to be afraid. God promised Joshua that He would be with him wherever he went. God is with us wherever we go, too. When we feel lonely or afraid it's helpful to remember that God is with us.

Joshua

Memory Verse

The Lord has surely given the whole land into our hands.
Joshua 2:24 (NIV)

For the Teacher

Using the patterns below, cut two cellophane or clear plastic circles and two rectangles of wrapping paper or adhesive-backed paper for each child. Provide two 4 ½-inch cardboard tubes, a 12-inch length of ribbon or wide elastic, a memory verse box, and a rubber band for each child.

Introduction

Forty years after Joshua had been a spy, he sent men into the land God promised to see how strong the people were. Joshua was not afraid because he believed that God would be with them and would help them conquer any enemy. The spies met a woman who said all of the people were afraid of the Israelites. When Joshua said, "Follow me," the people marched into the land God had waiting for them.

I Spy Binoculars

Cover two cardboard tubes with wrapping paper. Place glue on one end of each tube. Attach a circle of cellophane on each glued end to form a lens. Cut out the verse from below and glue it on one of the tubes. Wrap a rubber band around the tubes to hold them together. Your teacher will punch a hole near the end of one tube. Tie a piece of ribbon or elastic through the hole to form a hand strap for carrying the binoculars. If necessary, adjust the binoculars by pulling them apart slightly as you look through them.

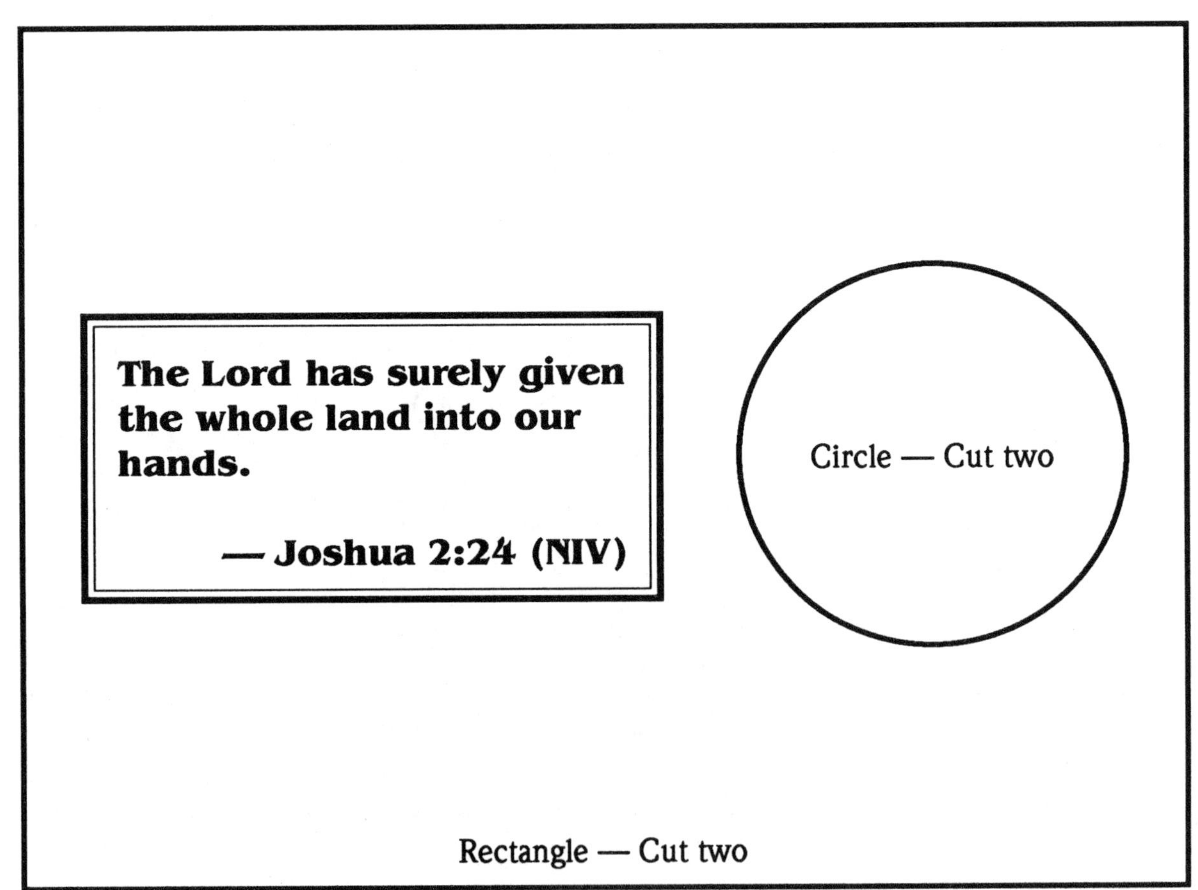

Memory Verse

The Lord said unto Joshua, "Fear not, neither be thou dismayed."
Joshua 8:1

For the Teacher

Duplicate the puppet patterns for each child. After the children cut out the puppets, punch holes as shown. Provide poster board, scissors, craft sticks, glue, paint brushes to spread the glue, crayons or markers, and four brass paper fasteners per child.

Introduction

To take over the land that God had promised, Joshua needed to capture a small town called Ai. He sent spies who reported that it would be easy to conquer this town. Joshua sent men to fight. They were defeated. Joshua asked God why they lost. God told him someone had sinned. Achan confessed to stealing gold, silver, and a coat. Joshua punished Achan. God then helped Joshua and his men win at Ai.

Joshua & Achan Puppets

Glue this page to a piece of poster board. Spread the glue with brushes to cover the puppet pieces completely. Cut out the puppet pieces and color them. Your teacher will punch holes in the puppet arms and legs. Attach the arms and legs to the bodies using brass paper fasteners to create your own Joshua and Achan characters. Glue a craft stick to the back of each puppet. Retell the Bible story using the puppets.

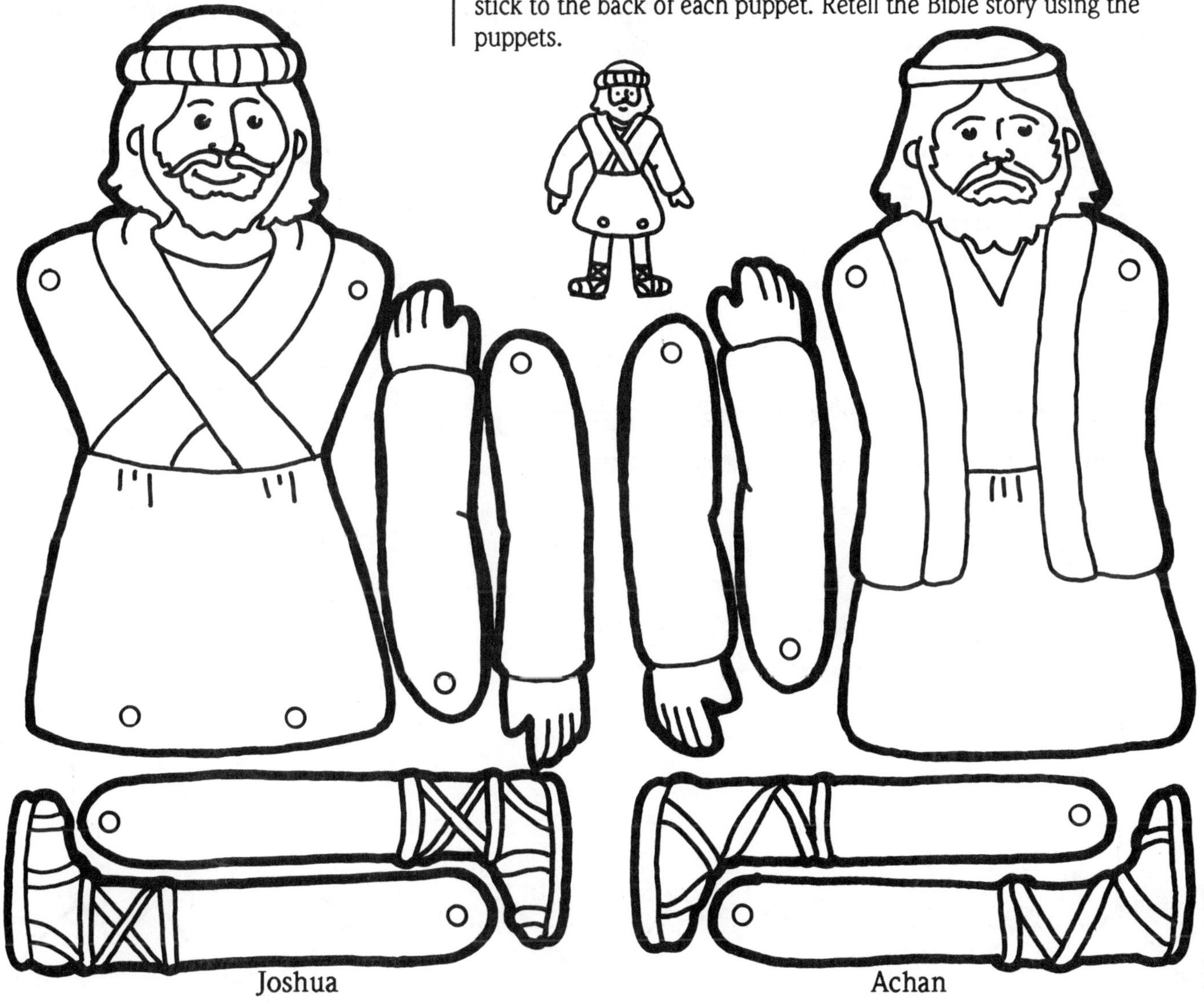

Joshua

Achan

Deborah

Memory Verse

God is...a very present help in trouble.
Psalm 46:1

For the Teacher

Provide a shoe box, bright construction paper, glue, scissors, and a garland pattern (below) for each child. NOTE: This stage is designed to be used with the Bible Hero Actors on page 13.

Introduction

The people of Israel disobeyed God and did what He said was wrong. God let the wicked King Jabin capture them. Jabin was cruel. The people cried for God to help. Deborah, Israel's judge, bravely told Barak that God would help them defeat Jabin's army. God confused the enemy. The Israelites won the battle.

Victory Stage

Cut off one long side of the shoe box. Cover the remaining sides of the box with bright paper. Trace the garland pattern several times onto a contrasting color of bright paper so it is the same length as the three sides of the box. Cut out the garland and glue it around the box.

Deborah

Memory Verse

*This is the day the Lord has given
Sisera into your hands.*
Judges 4:14 (NIV)

For the Teacher

Provide five paper clips, a magnet, glue, paint brushes to spread the glue, scissors, pattern pages 13 and 14, and construction paper for each child.

Introduction

God gave Deborah a plan to defeat evil King Jabin. She sent a message to Barak and told him God's commands. Instead of trusting God's battle plan, Barak told Deborah, "If you go with me, I will go; but if you don't go with me, I won't go." Deborah went with Barak to gather the soldiers. Because Barak would not follow God's orders, God would not let Barak be the one to capture Sisera. Instead, Sisera was defeated by Jael, a woman.

Bible Hero Actors

Glue the pattern page onto construction paper and cut out the figures. Fold each figure in half. Fold tabs A and B under. On each figure, glue tab A to tab B. Slip a paper clip (metal, not plastic) on the bottom of each figure. Stand the figures on the shoe box stage. Place a magnet under the stage floor and move the characters to recreate the Bible story.

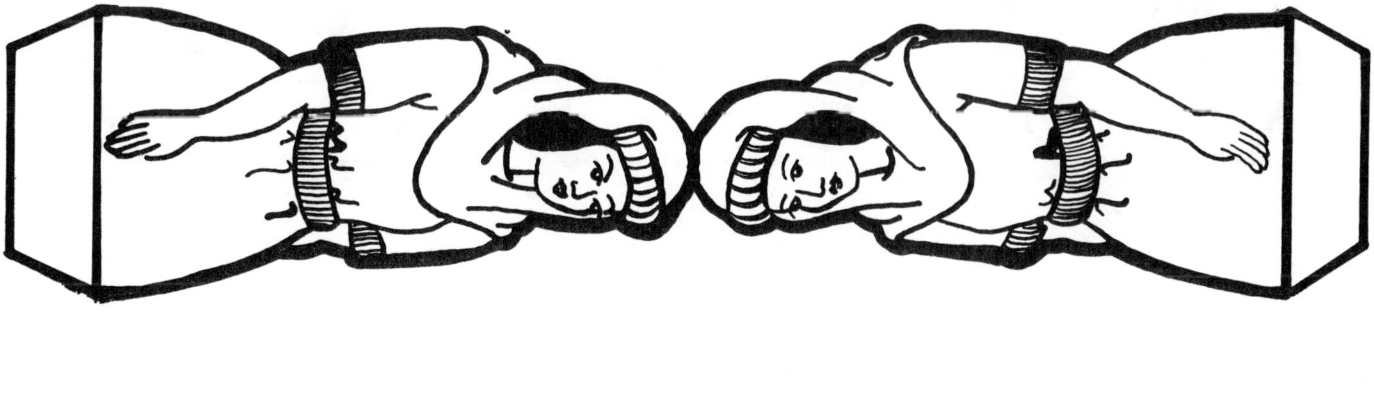

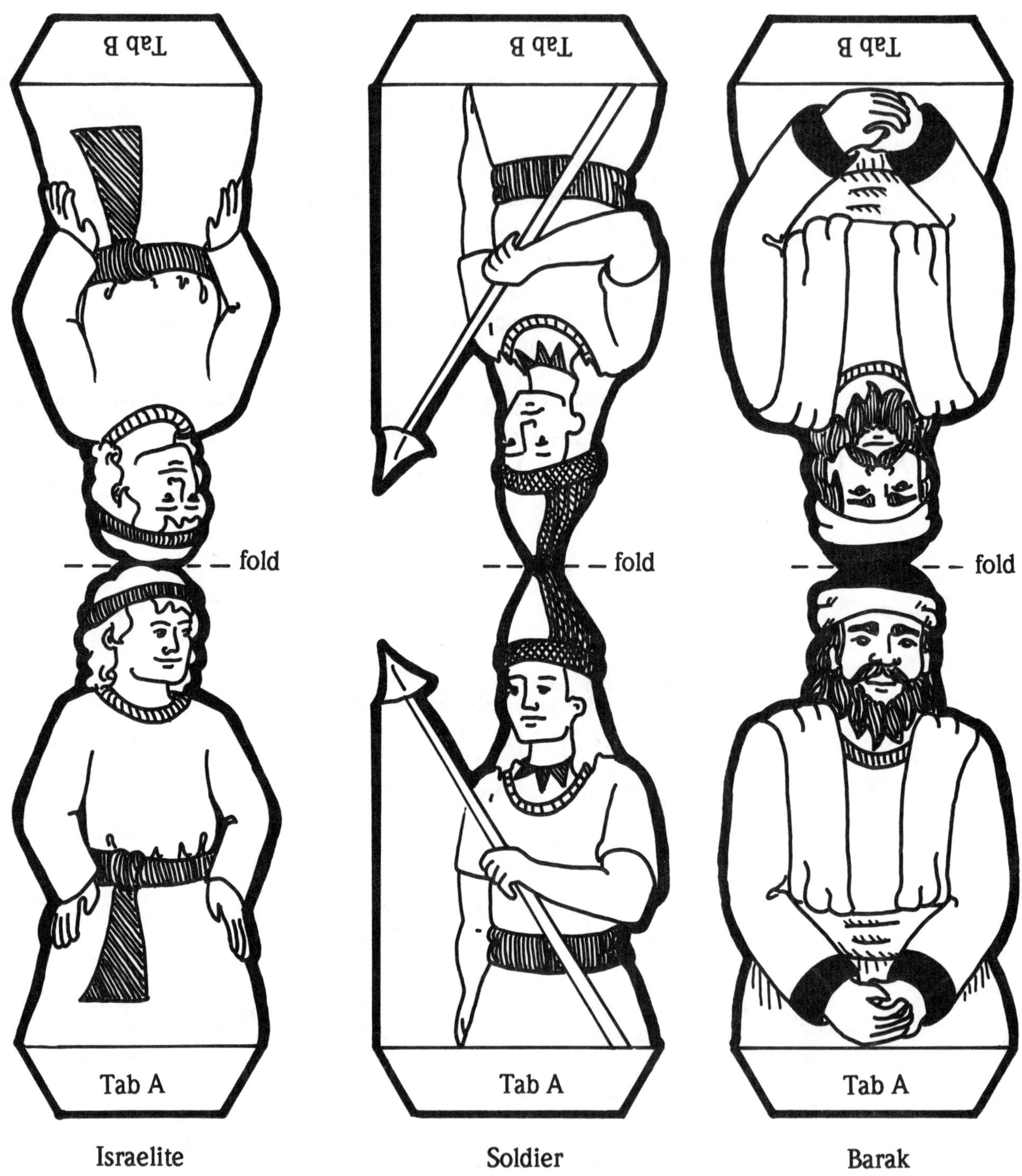

Favorite Bible Heroes for Grades 1 & 2

Deborah

Praising God
Judges 5

Memory Verse

I will make music to the Lord,
the God of Israel.
Judges 5:3 (NIV)

For the Teacher

Duplicate a pattern page for each child. Provide crayons. Talk about ways we thank God today. Sing a favorite song of praise together.

Introduction

Deborah was wise, strong, and brave. Deborah listened to God. Because Deborah obeyed God's plans for Israel, her people became stronger and stronger against their enemy. Deborah followed God, and the people followed Deborah. After they defeated King Jabin, the people sang a song thanking God for freeing them from an unkind enemy. They lived in peace for forty years.

Hidden Message Puzzle

To discover Deborah's message, color each space with a dot red. Color the remaining sections in other bright colors.

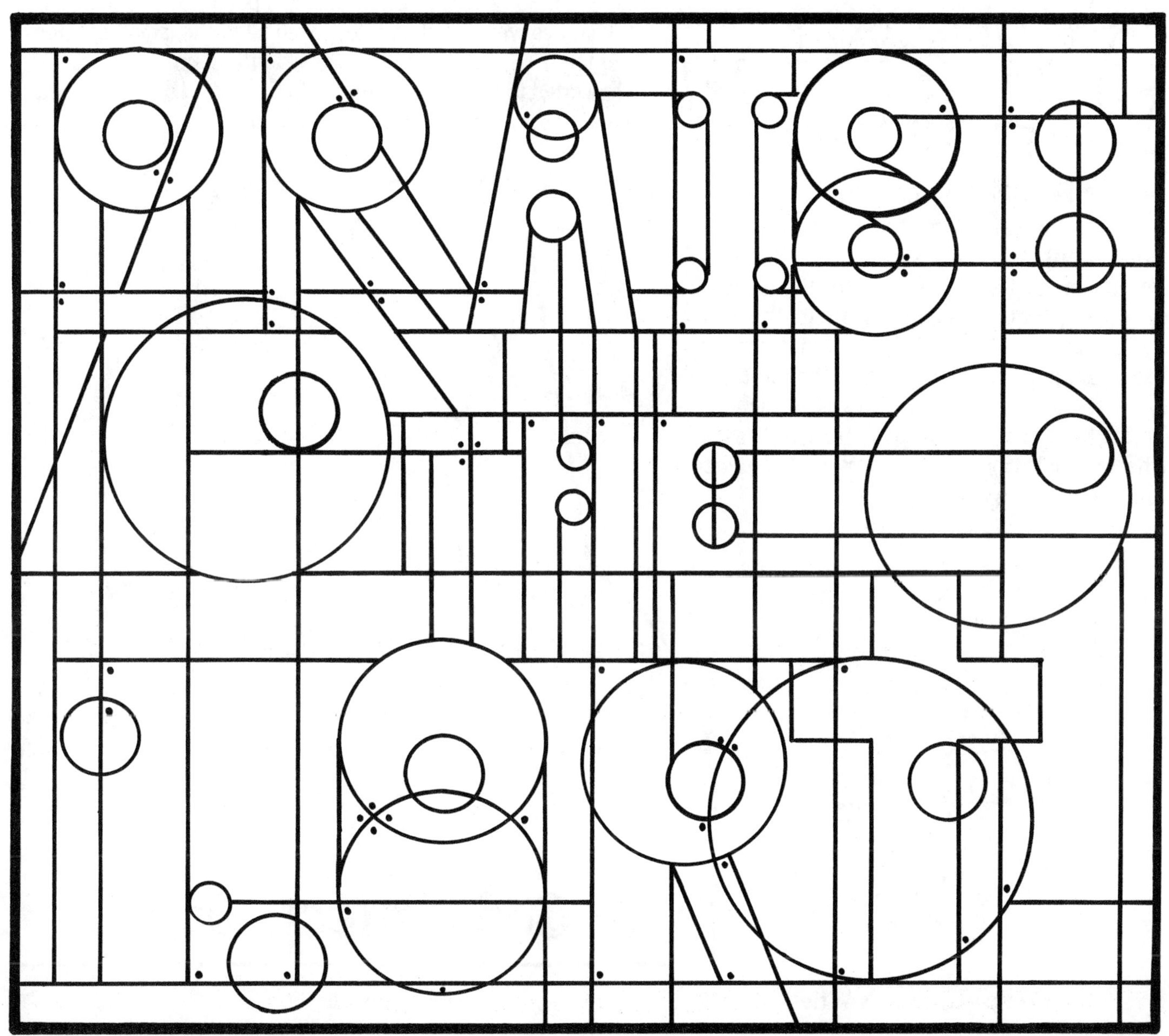

Gideon

Memory Verse
The Lord answered, "I will be with you."
Judges 6:16 (NIV)

For the Teacher
Duplicate pages 16 and 17. Cut out a Ferris wheel, stand, and seat pattern for each child. Provide bright poster board, scissors, pencils, and crayons or markers. Also bring five brass paper fasteners per child.

Introduction
The Israelites disobeyed God and did evil in the eyes of the Lord. So God gave the Midianites power over them. The Midianites were cruel and destroyed all of the Israelites' crops and food. To escape, the Israelites hid in mountain caves. They cried to God to help them. God sent them the prophet, Gideon, to rescue them from the enemy.

Ferris Wheel Protectors
Trace the Ferris wheel and stand onto bright poster board. Trace four seat patterns. Cut out all pieces. On each seat pattern, print the name of a person who protects you from harm (police officer, teacher, mom, dad, grandparent, God, Jesus, etc.). Use a brass paper fastener to secure the Ferris wheel to the stand. Then, secure each seat to the wheel. During the week, pray for each person on the Ferris wheel. Thank God for each person who protects you from harm.

Completed Ferris Wheel

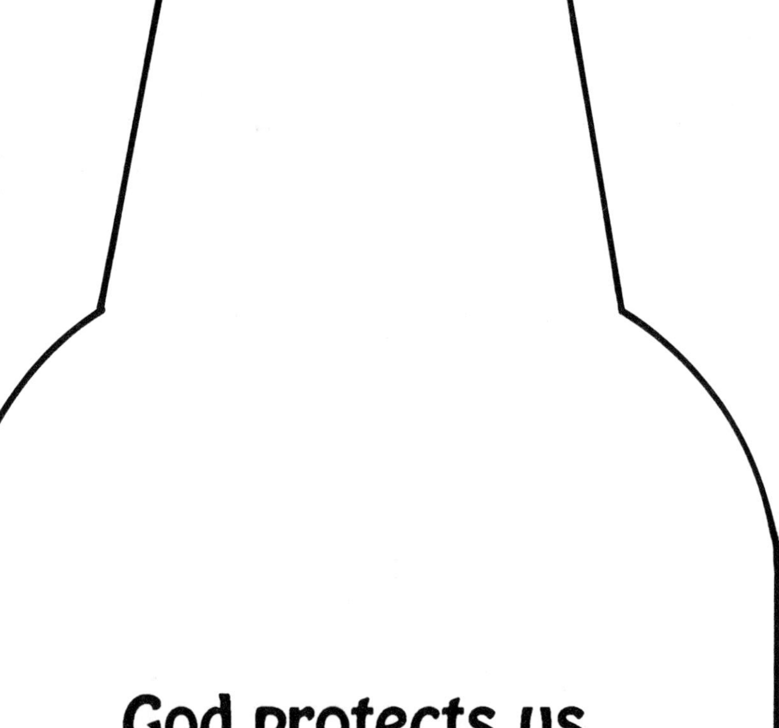

Stand

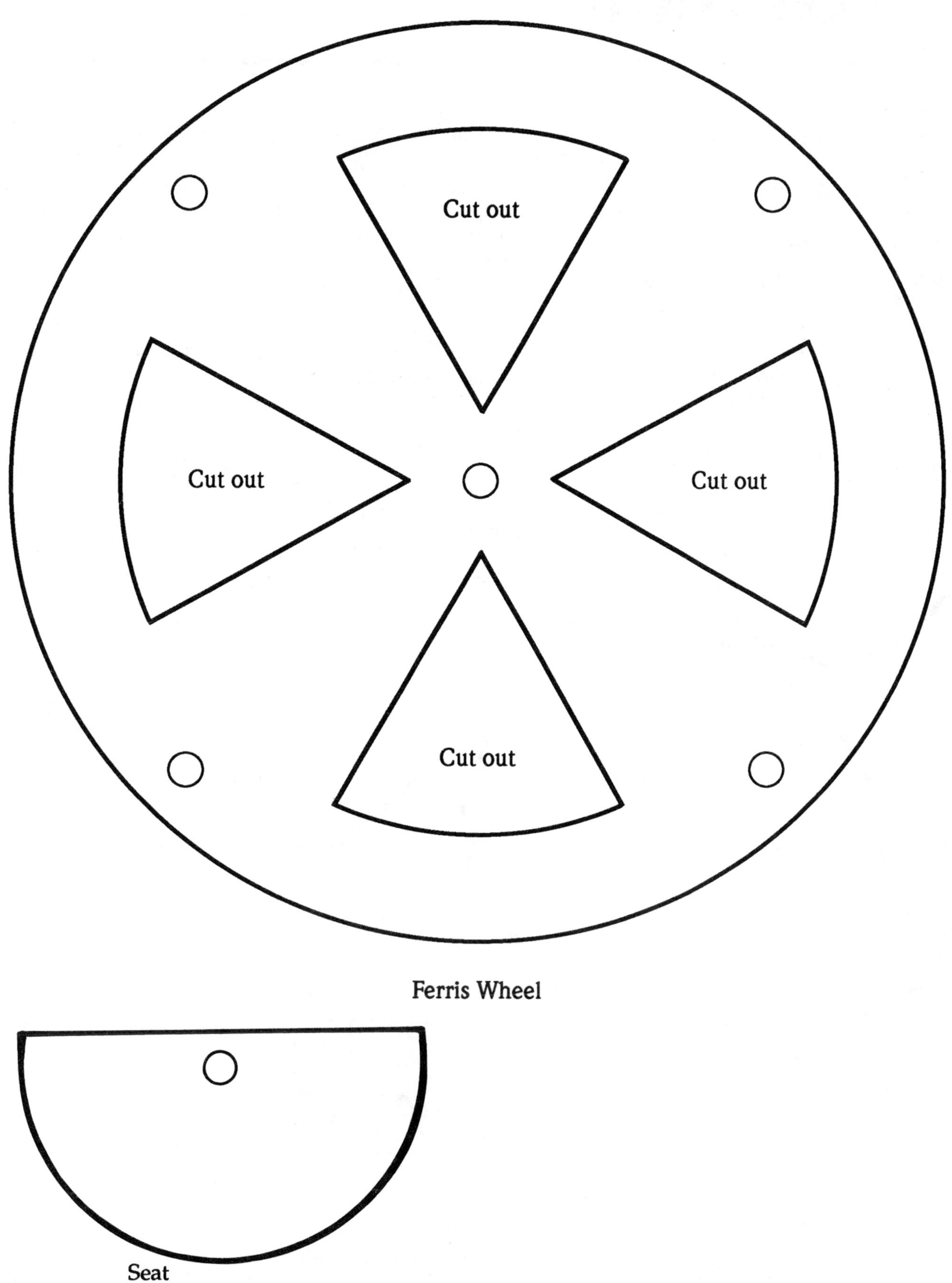

Ferris Wheel

Seat

Gideon

Face-to-Face with God's Angel
Judges 6:1-24

Memory Verse

*I have seen an angel of the Lord
face to face.*
Judges 6:22

For the Teacher

Duplicate an angel pattern for each child (fold the paper in half, lay the pattern on the fold, trace, cut out, and unfold). Provide scissors, paints or crayons, white poster board, yarn, and glue.

Introduction

An angel of the Lord appeared to Gideon. The angel told Gideon that the Lord was with him and he was a mighty warrior. Gideon didn't believe he could conquer the enemy. His family was weak and he was the youngest in his family. To be sure he understood what God was asking him to do, he asked God to show him a sign.

Angel Stand-Up Centerpiece

Cut out two angels from lightweight poster board. Paint or color all four sides with markers or crayons. Cut a 4 ½-inch slit from the bottom of one angel, and cut down 4 ½-inches from the top of the other angel. Glue yarn pieces for hair. Slip the pieces together to make the angel stand up.

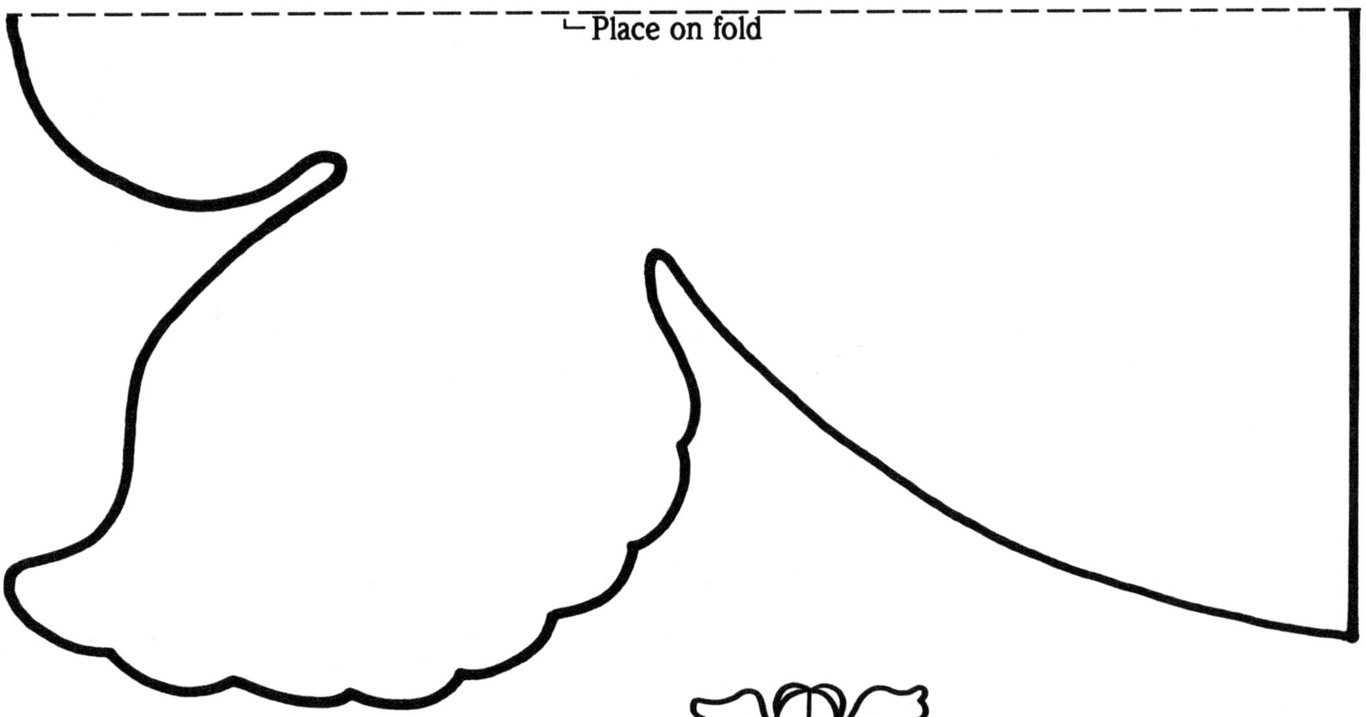

⌐ Place on fold

Completed Angel

Favorite Bible Heroes for Grades 1 & 2

Memory Verse

The Lord…rescued them from the hands of all their enemies.
Judges 8:34 (NIV)

For the Teacher

Duplicate this page for each child. Provide a shoe box, pencil, crayons, wrapping paper, glue, and stickers for each child. Cut a 4-inch wide piece of poster board ¼-inch less than the length of each shoe box. Let the children take turns narrating the story. Make additional reels for other Bible stories. The children may store their film reels in the shoe box.

Introduction

There were so many Midianites camped in a large valley that they could not be counted. In the middle of the night Gideon and his men surrounded them holding torches. The Israelites blew trumpets and shouted, "A sword for the Lord!" The Midianites tried to escape. But when the trumpet sounded, God made the Midianites fight each other with their swords! While Gideon was alive, Israel enjoyed peace for forty years.

At the Movies

Cover the sides of the shoe box with paper. Cut a ⅛ x 1-inch slit down the center of both long sides of the box to cradle a pencil to turn the film reel. Print the name of your theater on the poster board. Cut it in half. Glue a poster board half on each side of one slit, one inch down from the top of the box. One inch below the slit, cut a 1 ½-inch square for a movie screen. Glue the stage curtain around the screen. Decorate with stickers. Glue the film reel onto a 4 ¾-inch poster board circle. Draw the Bible story in the picture frames. Your teacher will punch a hole in the center of the film reel and push a pencil through it. Place the pencil in the cradle, line up the title frame, and turn the pencil to show the movie.

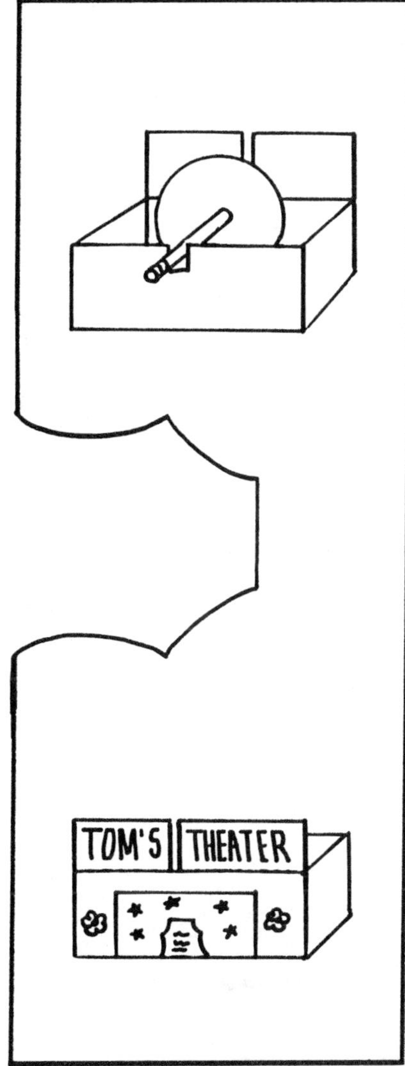

Curtain

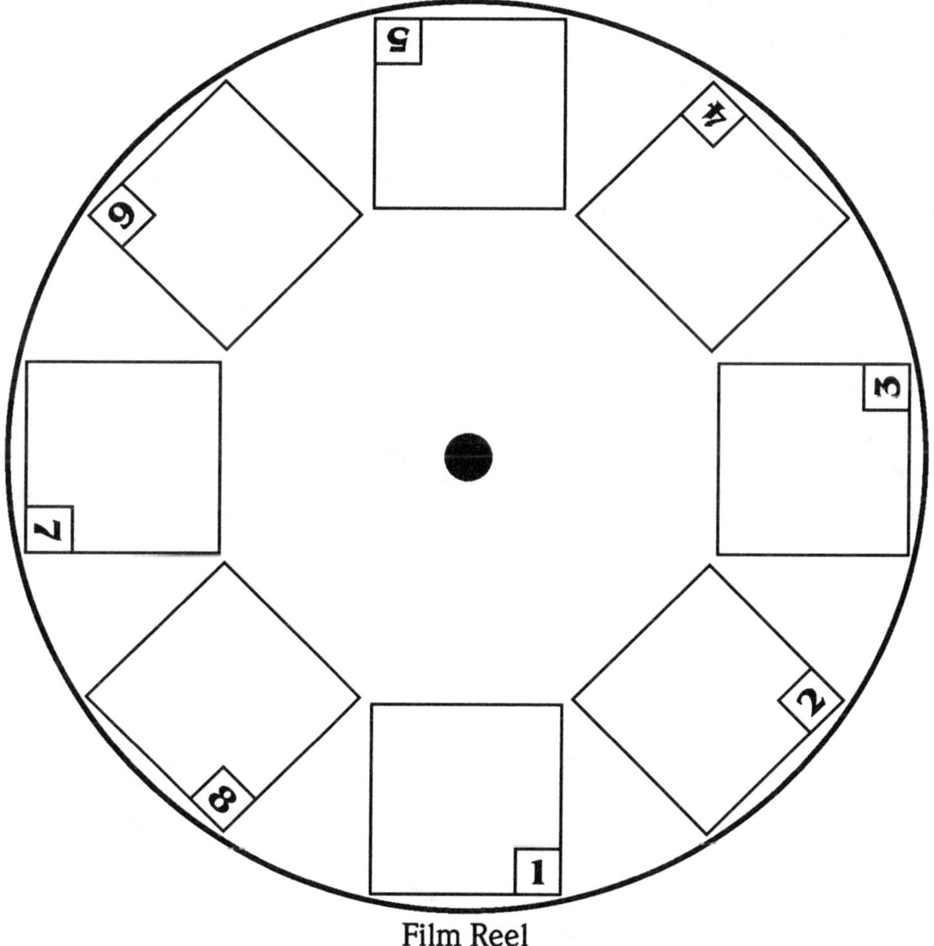

Film Reel

Ruth

Memory Verse

Your people will be my people and your God my God.
Ruth 1:16 (NIV)

For the Teacher

For each child, duplicate the spinner patterns, cut a 3 ½-inch cardboard circle, and tie two rubber bands together as shown on page 51. Provide scissors, glue, and markers or crayons. Help each child glue the patterns on the spinner so the words are directly behind each other.

Introduction

Naomi went with her husband to live in a wicked country called Moab. The Moabites worshipped other gods. Their two sons married Moabite women. When Naomi's husband and sons died, she decided to return to Israel. Naomi asked her daughters-in-law to go back to their homes. Ruth loved Naomi and her God, so she decided not to go back to her home. Instead, she stayed with Naomi.

Love God Spinner

Cut a 3 ½-inch cardboard circle. Cut out the circles below. Glue one on each side so the words are directly behind each other. Color both sides with crayons or markers. Your teacher will punch two holes. Thread the rubber band through each hole. Hold the spinner so LOVE faces you. Twist the ends of the rubber band back and forth and watch the spinner twirl. Read the message as the spinner twirls.

Completed Spinner

Ruth

Memory Verse

Always try to be kind to each other.
I Thessalonians 5:15 (NIV)

For the Teacher

Combine in a large bowl: one 16-ounce package granola cereal with raisins and dates, one 15-ounce package of hearty granola cereal, one 8-ounce package of chopped dried fruit, 1 cup of honey roasted peanuts, 1 cup chocolate covered raisins, and 1 cup chocolate covered peanuts. For each child, duplicate grain designs (or provide straw or hay), cut a 20-inch length of yarn, cut a 2 ¾ x 10-inch sheet of paper, and provide a 9-ounce paper or plastic cup. Also provide a hole punch, scissors, and glue.

Introduction

God had a plan to help women and children who had no food. He told farmers to pick the grain from their fields only once. What was left was for those who needed food. Ruth said to Naomi, "Let me go to the fields and pick up any leftover grain." Ruth was kind to Naomi and brought her food.

Harvest Basket

Glue paper to cover the cup sides. Then, glue grain stickers to the cup. Punch two holes opposite each other near the rim. Tie the yarn ends in the holes for a handle. "Glean" a granola snack and place it in your harvest basket.

Completed Basket

Ruth

Memory Verse

Blessed be thou of the Lord...for thou hast shown...kindness.
Ruth 3:10

For the Teacher

Duplicate this page for each child. For the bath oil mix 2 cups castile or baby shampoo, ¼ cup of safflower oil, and 2 teaspoons of lemon extract. Provide cinnamon sugar, glue bottles with narrow tips, cotton, scissors, a hole punch, and crayons or markers. Bring a jar with a screw top and a rubber band for each child. Cut fabric circles two inches larger than the jar lids, one for each child. Cut a ribbon long enough to encircle the jar diameter twice and tie a bow, one ribbon per child.

Introduction

Ruth worked very hard and picked grain in a field that was owned by Boaz. Boaz heard about many loving ways Ruth had been kind and thoughtful to Naomi. Boaz showed kindness to Ruth and gave her a meal, asked his men to pick and leave extra grain for Ruth, and protected her so no one could harm her.

Kindness Bubble Bath

Using a glue bottle, draw a heart or design on the side of the jar. Sprinkle cinnamon sugar over the glue. Glue three or four cotton balls to the top of the lid. Cut out the bath oil recipe and hearts and color them. Glue a cotton ball to one heart, and glue the other heart on top for a puffed look. Do the same with the other two hearts. Your teacher will punch a hole at the top of the hearts. Tie one end of a long ribbon to each heart. Fill the jar with bath oil. Screw the lid on the jar. Place the fabric circle over the lid. Slip a rubber band around the lid to hold the fabric in place. Tie the ribbon in a bow around the lid to cover the rubber band.

Bubble Bath

Contains the following ingredients:
2 cups castile or baby shampoo
¼ cup safflower oil
2 teaspoons lemon extract

Add a small amount to bath water, relax, and enjoy!

Memory Verse

The house of the righteous stands firm.
Proverbs 12:7 (NIV)

For the Teacher

Duplicate the house pattern. Cut the top off a ½-pint milk carton. Rinse well and dry. Provide four craft sticks, thin markers, glue, and scissors for each child. Use the patterns to cut four fabric robes for each child to glue on the craft sticks or let the children cut fabric or paper robes themselves.

Introduction

Naomi wanted Ruth to marry Boaz so Ruth would have a home and children. Naomi told Ruth to go to Boaz's field and do what he asked. Because Ruth loved and trusted Naomi, she obeyed. Boaz decided to marry Ruth. After they were married, God helped them have a baby boy named Obed. Obed was King David's grandfather.

A Home for Ruth & Boaz

With thin markers, color faces for Naomi, Ruth, Boaz, and Obed on craft sticks. Glue on clothes. Color the house, cut it out, and glue it to the milk carton. Place the stick puppets in the house and review the Bible story.

Solomon

Mother's Heart Pin

Glue a fabric square onto poster board. Trace a heart on the back of the poster board. Cut out the heart. Cut strips of material and ribbon. Glue fabric strips and small squares of fabric to the heart. For decoration, glue on tiny dried flowers, buttons, and beads. Attach a jewelry pin with an adhesive back to the back of the heart. Place the pin near the top of heart. Be careful to center the pin evenly between the sides of the heart. Show your love for a friend or relative by giving her this pin and saying, "I love you."

Memory Verse

The Lord loved him.
II Samuel 12:24

For the Teacher

Duplicate a heart pattern for each child. Cut an old pair of blue jeans or fabric into 4 x 4-inch squares. Provide poster board, glue, scissors, tiny dried or artificial flowers, ribbon, fabric scraps, buttons, beads, and a jewelry pin with an adhesive back or a safety pin for each child (use a hot glue gun to attach safety pins). Encourage the children to give the pin to their mothers or to an adult friend or relative to show their love for her.

Introduction

A baby boy was born to King David and his wife, Bathsheba. David named his son, Solomon. The Lord loved Solomon. Solomon was very special to the Lord. The Lord told Nathan the prophet to call the little boy, Jedidiah. The name Jedidiah means "loved by the Lord."

Solomon — Asking for Wisdom

I Kings 2:1-7; 3:5-15

Memory Verse

God gave Solomon wisdom and understanding.
I Kings 4:29

For the Teacher

Duplicate this page for each child. Provide paper clips, scissors, pencils, crayons or markers, and tape. As the children work, talk about how Solomon showed his love for God. Help the children think of ways they can show love for God, too.

Introduction

David told Solomon to be a good, strong leader; obey God; follow His rules; and be kind to his friends. In a dream, God told Solomon, "Ask for whatever you want Me to give you." Instead of asking for money or long life, Solomon asked for strength to obey and wisdom to know the difference between right and wrong. The Lord was pleased with Solomon for making such a good choice.

Wisdom Tree

Fold three pieces of 9 x 12-inch construction paper in half lengthwise. Cut out the wisdom tree pattern. Stack the sheets of folded construction paper on top of each other. Paper clip the wisdom tree pattern securely to the fold. Trace and/or cut out the wisdom tree on all three sheets of folded construction paper. Open the trees and tape the folds together. On the tree print some of the following phrases: "Obey God," "God gives wisdom," "God is kind," "God gives good gifts," "God is Good," "God loves (your name)."

Place on the fold

Solomon

Building the Temple
I Kings 6:1-9:5

Memory Verse

Blessed be the Lord God of Israel.
I Kings 8:15

For the Teacher

Using a graham cracker as a guide, cut off the top of a cleaned and dried ½-pint milk carton for each child. Each child also will need a plastic knife, five graham crackers, a dessert-size paper plate, a plastic drinking straw, frosting, marshmallows, and colored candy. Cover the work area with paper. Have paper towels handy for clean-up. Put smocks (men's short-sleeved shirts) on the children. Mix 2 pounds of confectioners' sugar, 6 egg whites at room temperature, and 1 teaspoon cream of tartar in a large bowl. Mix on low speed until the ingredients are moist. Then mix on high speed for seven minutes or until the frosting makes stiff peaks when a knife is pulled through it. Keep the frosting covered. It dries quickly. This recipe makes 4 cups. Each Temple-Church will need about ½ cup of frosting.

Introduction

The Lord gave Solomon wisdom to build a temple where people could go to worship God. It took the workers and craftsmen seven years to complete the inside and outside of the building. Solomon thanked God and asked Him to hear their prayers. God promised Solomon that His eyes and heart would always be in the temple if Solomon and his sons obeyed God.

Graham Cracker Temple-Church

Turn a milk carton upside down on a sturdy dessert-size paper plate. Place a dab of frosting on all four corners of the carton and stick it to the paper plate. Place a small amount of frosting on the back of five graham crackers and affix them to the carton top and sides. Using a knife or fingers, spread frosting along the seams. Make a door with frosting. Then decorate the Temple-Church with marshmallows and colored or metallic candies. Cut a plastic drinking straw to form pillars around the temple door.

Completed Temple

Solomon

Memory Verse

Your hearts must be fully committed to the Lord our God, to…obey His commands.
I Kings 8:61 (NIV)

For the Teacher

Provide a plastic spray can lid and a pencil or dressmaker's chalk for each child. Also bring silk flowers, beads, ribbon, and fabric or wrapping paper. Place the spray can lid on cardboard or poster board and trace around it. Cut out the cardboard and trim it to fit inside the rim of the lid.

Introduction

Solomon was famous all over the world. People came to his court to hear the wisdom God had put in Solomon's heart. The Queen of Sheba heard about Solomon's wisdom and love for God. She wanted to test him. She asked him many questions. No question was too hard for him to answer. The queen was very surprised by his answers and the beautiful temple he had built. She praised God and gave Solomon gold, spices, and precious stones.

Ring Gift Box

Glue fabric or gift wrap around the side of the spray can lid. Lay the cardboard circle on fabric or wrapping paper and trace around it. Cut it out and glue it on top of the cardboard. Trim the top with a silk flower, a bead, or a ribbon bow. This box makes a good place to keep your rings. Remember wise Solomon when you use it.

HINT: Dilute white glue with a small amount of water. It will spread easily and will dry quicker. Use paint brushes to spread glue.

Completed Ring Box

Elisha

Prophet of God
1 Kings 19:1-21

Memory Verse
He did what the Lord had told him.
I Kings 17:5 (NIV)

For the Teacher
Duplicate pages 28 and 29 for each child. Glue the code wheels to a sheet of construction paper, one sheet per child. Duplicate the coded message for each child. Provide pencils or crayons, scissors, and brass paper fasteners.

Introduction
God told Elijah the prophet to go stand on a mountain and the Lord would pass by. A strong wind came and made the mountain fall apart before Elijah's eyes. Then an earthquake and a fire came. God was not in the wind, earthquake, or fire. Then Elijah heard a whisper. The Lord told Elijah to pour oil on Elisha's head. God planned for Elisha to take Elijah's place as a prophet.

Decoding Wheel
Cut out the two code wheels. Place the smaller alphabet code wheel on top of the larger wheel. Insert a brass paper fastener in the center. Move the wheels until the arrow lines up with the letter E. Then, decode the message about Elisha. Use the code wheel to make your own secret message.

Secret Message

Begin with arrow ⬆ at E.

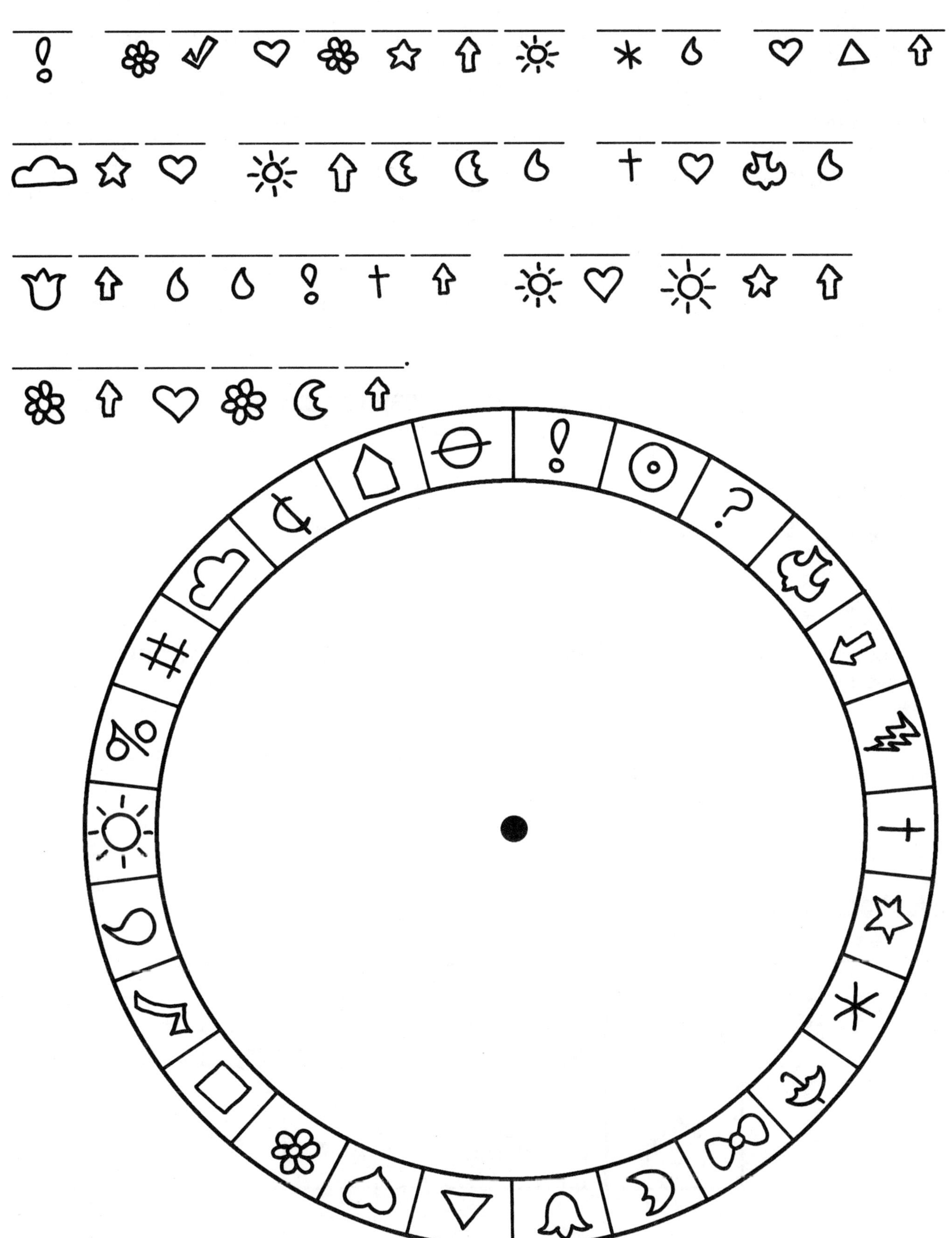

Elisha

Watching Elijah Go to Heaven
II Kings 2:9-17

Memory Verse
The spirit of Elijah is resting on Elisha.
II Kings 2:15 (NIV)

For the Teacher
Duplicate this page for each child. Provide crayons or markers, scissors, and glue.

Introduction
Elijah asked Elisha what he could do for him before the Lord took Elijah away. Elisha wanted to inherit a double portion of Elijah's spirit. If Elisha would watch as Elijah was taken away to heaven, then the spirit Elijah had would be his. Elisha watched as a chariot and horses made of fire took Elijah away to heaven in a whirlwind. Elisha picked up Elijah's coat. He hit the river water with the coat, and the river parted. Elisha walked back across the river on dry ground. The people who watched said, "The spirit of Elijah now rests on Elisha."

Whirlwind Chariot Picture Story
Cut apart the pictures. Glue each picture in place to complete the story.

Elijah told Elisha to watch as he was taken away to heaven. Then the spirit of

Elijah would be Elisha's. A   and   made

of   took Elijah away in a whirlwind. Elisha picked up

Elijah's   . He hit the   with the   .

He walked across the river on   .

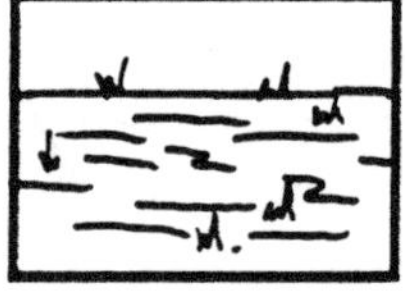   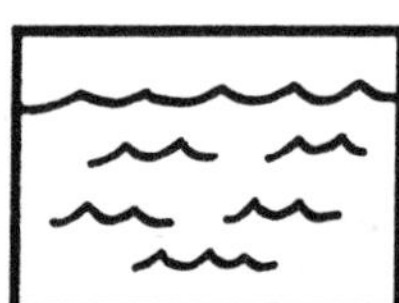

Favorite Bible Heroes for Grades 1 & 2

Helping a Worried Mother
II Kings 4

Memory Verse

My help comes from the Lord, the Maker of heaven and earth.
Psalm 121:2 (NIV)

For the Teacher

Prepare peanut butter clay dough and divide it into ⅓-cup portions. The recipe below makes enough for ten children. Provide a dinner-size paper plate for each child. As the children make their pots, talk about how Elisha took care of the woman. Explain that God takes care of our needs, too.

Introduction

A single mother didn't have the money she needed to pay a man to whom she owed money. This man wanted to take her two sons to be his slaves. Frightened, the mother asked Elisha for help. Elisha said, "Gather all your neighbor's jars. Pour oil in each jar." Oil filled the jars. Elisha said, "Sell the oil, then pay the man." After the woman paid the man, there was even money left over.

Peanut Butter Clay Pots

Help the children wash and dry their hands. Give each child a dinner-size paper plate and ⅓ cup of clay dough to shape into jars and pots. Children can eat their jars immediately or take them home on their plates to eat as a snack after their meal.

Completed Pots

Peanut Butter Clay Dough

2 cups creamy peanut butter
1 ¾ cups honey
3 cups nonfat powdered milk
1 cup flour

Put peanut butter in a bowl. Add honey and powdered milk alternately. Mix each thoroughly before adding more. If the clay is too sticky, keep adding flour until the dough is dry enough to shape.

Ezra

Servant of God

Ezra 1; 7

For the Teacher

For each child, duplicate this page, paint an empty thread spool light tan, and provide a sharpened pencil, a large round lollipop (not flat), a 10-inch length of yarn, and a 6-inch square of light-colored solid fabric or muslin.

Introduction

The Israelites did not love God. God watched as they did evil things. God let the Babylonians destroy the temple and tear down all the walls around Jerusalem. They captured the Israelites and took them to Babylon to become servants. Many years later, the king of Persia freed the Israelites (now called Jews) to return to Jerusalem. Ezra wanted to teach them about God's rules. King Artaxerxes was so impressed by Ezra's love for God that he helped pay for Ezra to take some of the Jews home to Israel.

HINT: Add a few drops of dishwashing soap to tempera paint and it will paint on shiny surfaces such as foil, glass, or plastic. It will also wash out of clothes more easily.

King & Ezra Puppets

King: Trace a crown onto lightweight poster board. Glue sequins or stars to the crown. Glue the crown around the top of the spool. Draw a face on the spool. Glue a collar around the bottom of the spool. Glue cotton balls to the bottom edge of the spool. Place glue on the sharpened end of a pencil and push the tip into the hole in the bottom of the spool.

Ezra: Place a square of fabric over a large round lollipop. Tie yarn around the neck. Draw on a face. Glue a headpiece to the top of the head.

Use your puppets to tell the story of Ezra.

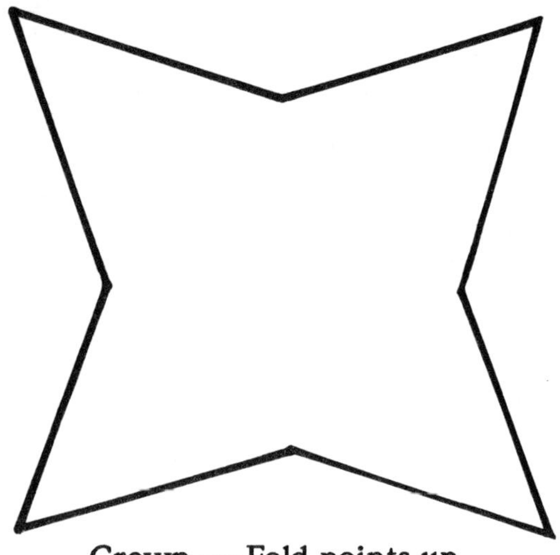

Crown — Fold points up

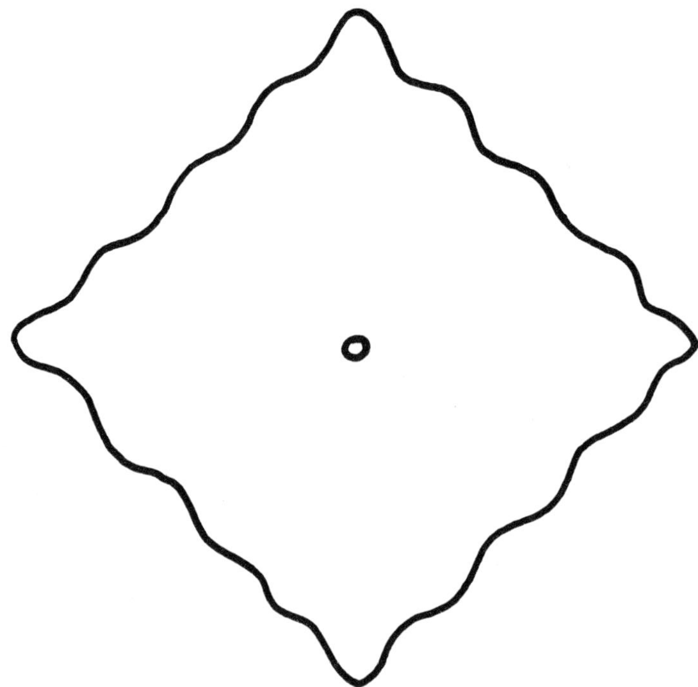

Collar — Fold points down

Ezra

Memory Verse

*Humble ourselves before our God and
ask Him for a safe journey.*
Ezra 8:21 (NIV)

For the Teacher

For each child, duplicate pages 33 and
34 four or five times. Provide poster board
or lightweight cardboard, clear adhesive-
backed plastic, scissors, glue, crayons or
markers, and a plastic sandwich bag for
each child.

Introduction

It was a long, dangerous trip back to Jerusalem. Ezra worried
about the Jews' safety. Ezra was too embarrassed to ask the king for
soldiers to protect them. He had told Artaxerxes that God helps those
who obey Him. Ezra prayed. He asked God for a safe trip for the Jews,
their children, and their possessions. God answered Ezra's prayers.

Bingo Car Game

Glue bingo cards to poster board or lightweight cardboard and cut
them out. Color the pictures and cut them out. Glue them to the
squares on each card, so each card is different. Cover the cards with
clear adhesive-backed plastic. Store them in a plastic sandwich bag. To
play, give a card to each player. Mark the card with a washable
marker each time you see one of the pictures. The first player to find
all the pictures on one row wins. Wipe off the cards and play again.
Remember, God is with you wherever you go.

Ambulance

Railroad
Tracks

Grocery Store

Bicycle

Dog

FREE

Sun

House

Motorcycle

Movie
Theater

Mini-Van

Mobile Home

Baby

Sports Car

Billboard

Stop Sign

Yield Sign

Stop Light

Gas Station

Fire Truck

Police Car

Church

Pine Tree

Flower

Pick-up Truck

CAR BINGO

Ezra

Doing God's Will
Ezra 1-7

Memory Verse

Ezra had prepared his heart to seek the law of the Lord and to do it.
Ezra 7:10

For the Teacher

For each child, cut a 6 x 12-inch piece of muslin and cut a star from the side of a clean milk carton or from foam, using the pattern below. Bring a spool for each child.

Introduction

In Babylon, the Israelites ate different food, learned a new language, Aramaic, and forgot how to speak Hebrew. They didn't have a temple where they could worship God. Some people think Ezra began a synagogue to help the Jews remember God. Ezra was called the "Father of Judaism." Some people believe Ezra may have dictated 24 Old Testament books from memory so God's teachings would not be lost.

Star of David Scroll

Glue the star onto the top of an empty thread spool. Use a marker to draw an arrow on the bottom of the spool to indicate the top of the star. Spread glue along the edge of one 6-inch end of the muslin your teacher gives you. Place a small wooden dowel or a new pencil on the glue and let it dry. When the glue has dried on the spool, dip the star in tempera paint and make designs across the scroll.

Completed Scroll

Daniel

Memory Verse

As for me and my house, we will serve the Lord.
Joshua 24:15

For the Teacher

Duplicate the crown and gem patterns from pages 36 and 37 for each child. Provide scissors, 18 x 24-inch construction paper, glue, foil, metallic wrapping paper, star stickers, and crayons or pencils. When crowns are finished, staple the ends of the crown to fit the children's heads. Cover the staples with tape to prevent scratching.

Introduction

Captured by King Nebuchadnezzer, Daniel was taken to Babylon. Daniel trusted God to protect him from harm. He was a teenager, but he loved and obeyed God. Nebuchadnezzer chose Daniel, Shadrach, Meshach, and Abednego to serve him. They found favor with the king because God gave them more knowledge and wisdom than all the king's fortune tellers.

Making Good Choices Crown

Fold an 18 x 24-inch construction paper sheet in half. Lay the crown pattern on the fold and trace. Cut out crown and gem pieces from various colors of construction paper, foil, or metallic wrapping paper. Glue gems or stars to the crown for decoration. Color the crown with markers.

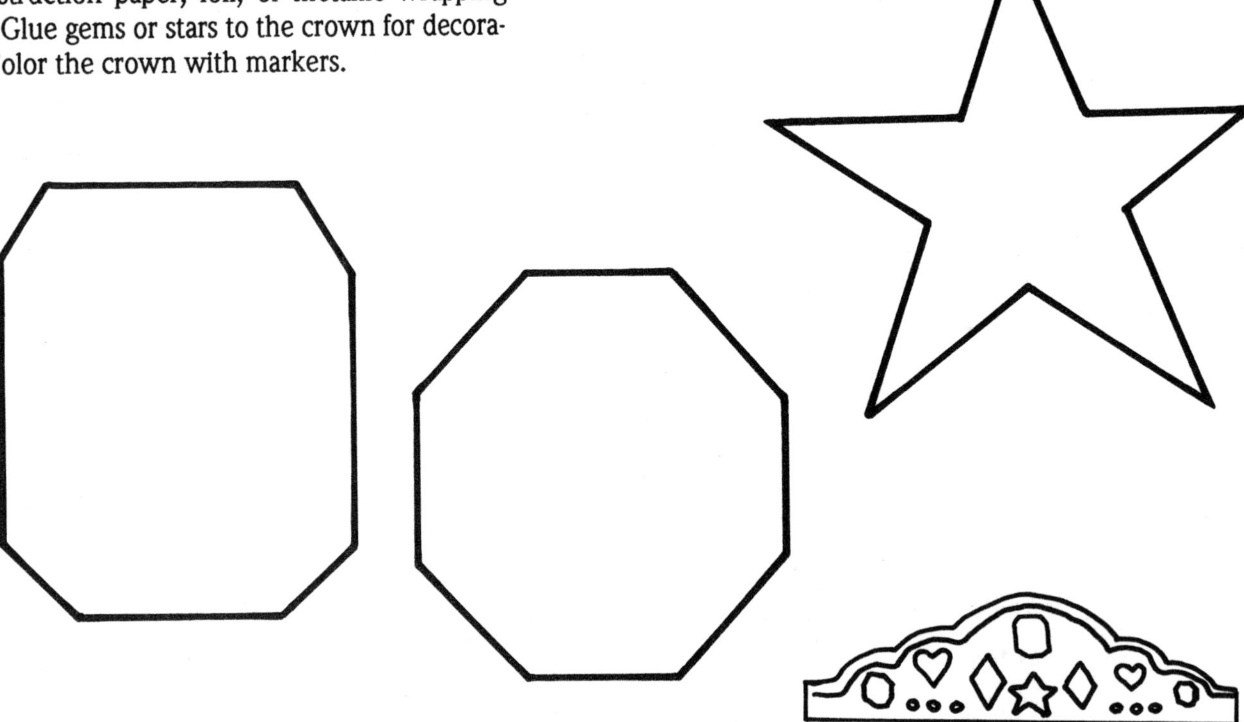

Completed Crown

Place on fold

Daniel

Memory Verse

*The Lord works out everything for
His own ends.*
Proverbs 16:4 (NIV)

For the Teacher

For each child, duplicate a face and eye pattern. Provide brass paper fasteners, poster board, scissors, and crayons or markers. Cut a 3 ¾-inch poster board circle for each child. Punch a hole in the middle of each circle.

Introduction

King Nebuchadnezzer made a tall gold statue and ordered everyone to worship it. Daniel's friends, Shadrach, Meshach, and Abednego, refused to obey the king's orders. They, like Daniel, obeyed God's orders not to worship other gods. The king was angry when these three young men refused to do what he wanted, so he threw them into a fiery furnace. King Nebuchadnezzer didn't believe that any god could protect them. Imagine how surprised the king was when he looked into the furnace and saw four, not three, figures. The surprised king admitted that God protected the men from harm.

Hot Under the Collar King

Glue the king's head onto poster board, cut it out, and color it. Color and cut out the eyes and glue them onto the poster board circle your teacher gives you (place the eyebrows closest to the circle edge). Attach the face and eye pieces with a brass paper fastener. Turn the eyes to show the king's changing expressions as you tell the story from the king's point of view.

 # Daniel

Trusting God and Doing His Will
Daniel 6

Memory Verse

My God sent His angel and He shut the mouths of the lions.
Daniel 6:22 (NIV)

For the Teacher

Duplicate this page for each child. Provide pencils or crayons.

Introduction

When King Nebuchadnezzar died, the new king decided to put Daniel in charge of the kingdom. This made some people very jealous. They asked the king to make a rule that anyone who prayed to any god but the king would be thrown in the lions' den. When Daniel prayed to God, they reported him. The king hoped that Daniel's God would protect him from the hungry lions. Because Daniel trusted God, his life was saved.

Daniel & the Lions Puzzle

Draw a line from each lion above a letter to the matching lion below. Write the letter in the blank of the matching lion. The answer will spell the name of the new king who took over when Nebuchadnezzar died (Daniel 5:31). This king was glad that God was able to save Daniel from the lions.

R   D   S   A   I   U

John the Baptist

Memory Verse

And you, my child, will be called a prophet of the Most High.
Luke 1:76 (NIV)

For the Teacher

Cut a 6 x 18-inch piece of construction paper for each child. Accordion fold the paper every three inches to form six door panels. Open the paper. Duplicate this page for each child. As the children work, encourage them to show the door to a friend or family member. Suggest that they guess who is behind the door before opening it.

Introduction

An angel surprised Zechariah with the news that he would have a son named John. God promised John would come to prepare the Jews for the coming of Jesus. Because Zechariah didn't believe God's message, Zechariah was unable to talk until the baby was born. After the baby was born, Zechariah wrote John's name on a tablet. Instantly, he could speak again. Zechariah praised God.

Secret Door Surprise

Lay flat the construction paper your teacher gives you. Using the door diagram, draw a door on the first five sections, each one smaller than the one before it. Cut the doors on three sides, as shown. Do not fold the doors open. Fold the construction paper back into an accordion. Glue together the top and bottom edges of each page. Open the doors. Draw a picture of John or print his name behind the last door. Decorate the front of each door. Glue the memory verse on the first door. Show the door to a friend.

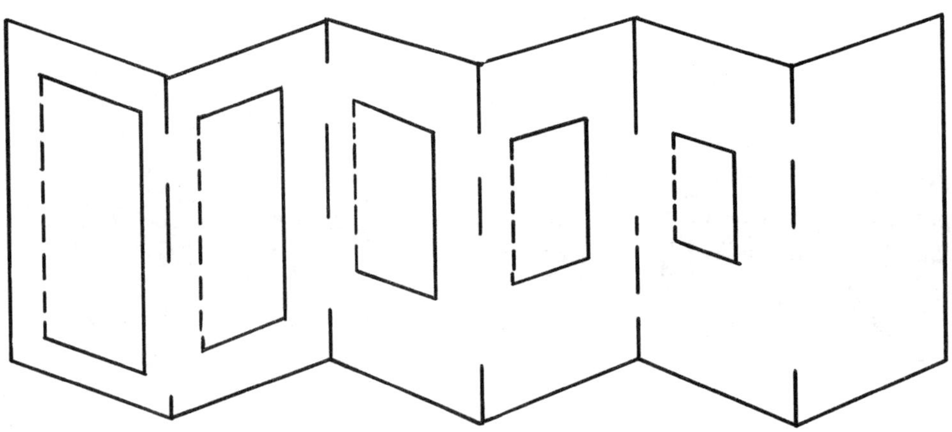

Door Diagram
Cut on solid lines.

And you, my child, will be called a prophet of the Most High.

Luke 1:76(NIV)

John the Baptist

Memory Verse

Prepare ye the way of the Lord, make His paths straight.
Luke 3:4

For the Teacher

Provide honey, butter, cinnamon, bread, plastic knives, scissors, plates, napkins, bowls and spoons for mixing, a 1-cup measuring cup, a ½-teaspoon measuring spoon, and a toaster oven (or several). Duplicate the recipe for each child.

Introduction

When John became a man, he lived in the desert, ate locusts and wild honey, and wore clothes made of camel's hair. Many people came to the desert to hear him preach. He told them to change their minds about doing wrong. God would forgive them if they would love Him. Many people were sorry for their wrong actions and choices. They decided to obey God.

Honey Bread

Mix the ingredients to make honey butter. Spread honey butter on the bread. Place the bread in a toaster oven until bubbly. Talk about John's message as the bread cools. Cut out a recipe card to take home. Thank God for John the Baptist and for good food. Then, eat and enjoy!

John the Baptist

Good News
Luke 3:7-18; Matt. 3:7-11

Memory Verse

John...preached the Good News to them.
Luke 3:18

For the Teacher

Duplicate this page for each child. Provide 5 x 8-inch and 3 x 5-inch unlined index cards, glue, crayons, a hole punch, scissors, yarn or ribbon, fabric scraps, gift wrap, holiday cards, stickers, etc. After children fold the cards, punch a hole in the upper left-hand corner of each.

Introduction

People asked John to tell them ways to show love for God. John said share your clothes and food with those who have less, don't take money that doesn't belong to you, tell the truth, and be happy with what you have. He made peace between parents and children and told fathers to love their children. People wondered if John might be Jesus. As God had planned, John said Jesus was coming.

Think of Others Note Cards

Fold two index cards in half. Cut shapes from the patterns below or from fabric, gift wrap, cards, and stickers and glue them on the front of the cards. Insert a 6-inch length of yarn or ribbon in the hole punched in each card and tie. Glue a message on the inside or print one of your own. Print your name at the bottom. Attach the cards to gifts or give them to parents or friends.

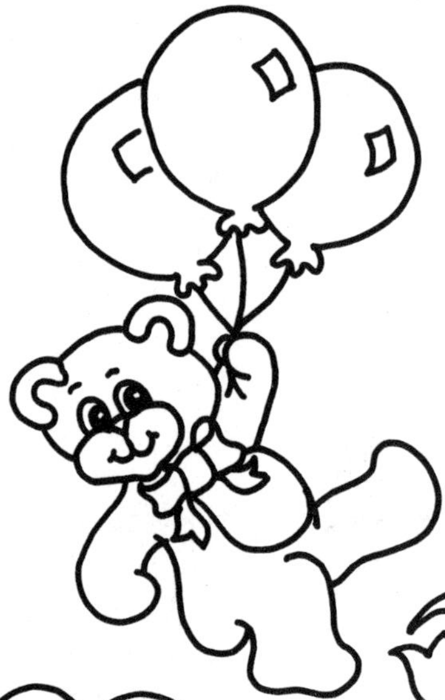
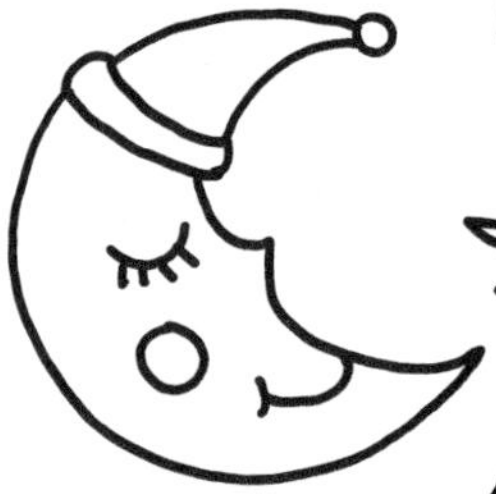
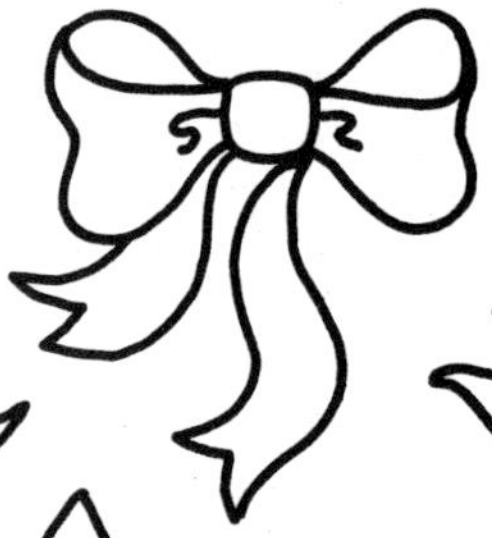
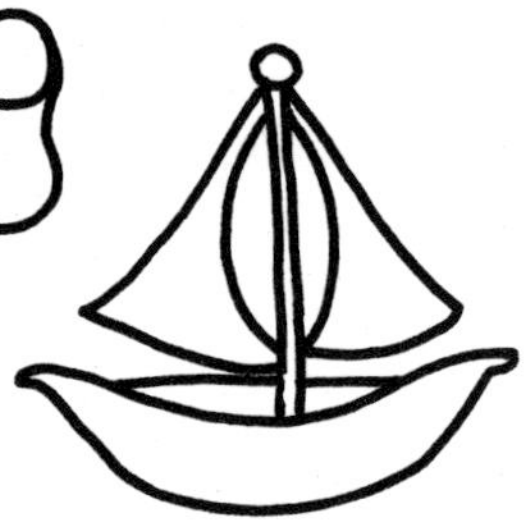
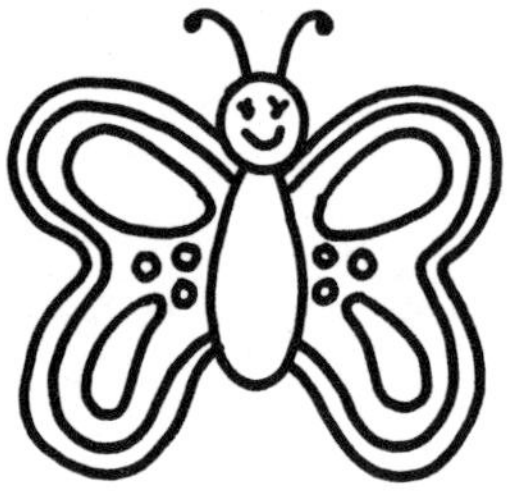
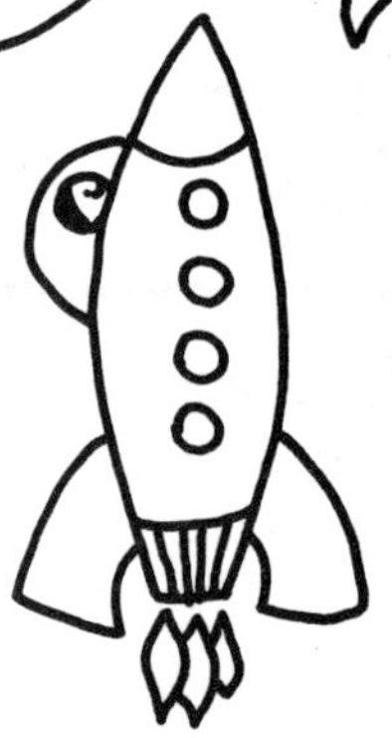
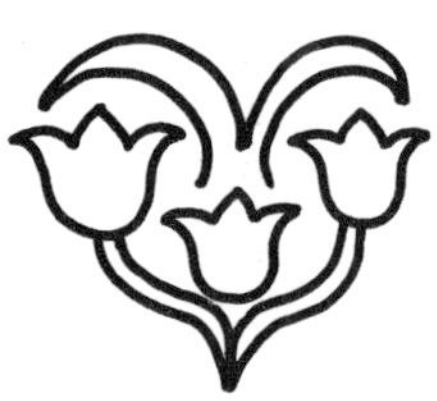
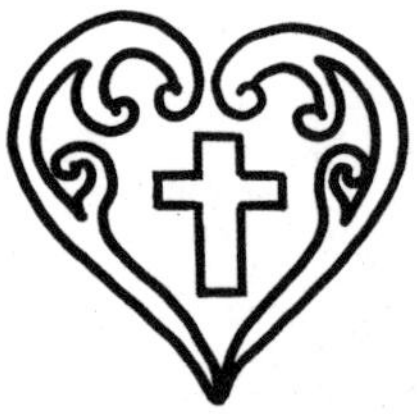
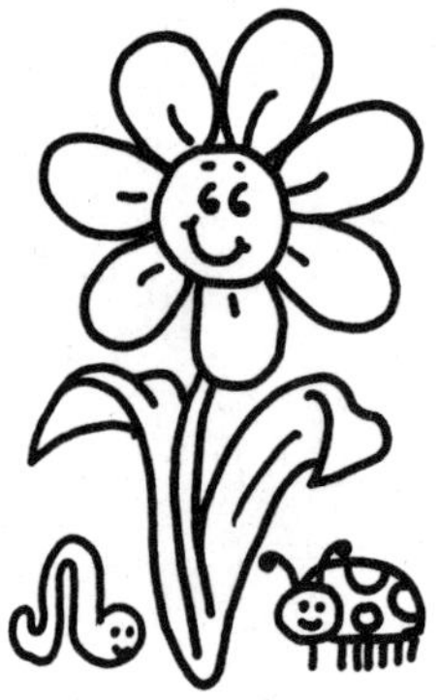

You're special!

I'm thinking of YOU!

Memory Verse

And a voice came from heaven, which said, "Thou art My beloved Son."
Luke 3:22

For the Teacher

Bring a pitcher of water, a glass, a shiny penny, vinegar, a tablespoon, paper towels, and a tarnished penny for each child. Pour water into the glass to fill it half way. Add 3 tablespoons of vinegar.

Introduction

People who showed everyone they wanted to follow God were baptized. John would dip them under the water of the Jordan River. One day, Jesus asked John to baptize Him. John knew Jesus was God's Son. John asked, "Why do You want me to baptize You? I need to be baptized by You." Jesus said it was God's will. As John was bringing Jesus out of the water, the Holy Spirit came down like a dove and God's voice said, "This is My Son. I love Him. I am pleased with Him."

New Life Pennies & Puzzle

Look at your dirty, tarnished penny. Compare it to the shiny penny your teacher has. Drop your penny into the glass and stir for ten seconds. Take the penny out of the water and dry it. Notice the penny is clean and shiny. When we ask Jesus to forgive our sins, He forgets our sins. The shiny penny represents the way God wants our lives to be. The people who asked John to baptize them were telling others they had decided to stop making wrong choices and were ready to live brand new lives.

Color all the boxes below that contain the letters Q, X, or Z. Write the letter that remains in each column in the box directly below that column. The answer will be the Bible Hero who said, "I baptize you with water."

Q	Z	Z	Q	T	Z	Z	Q	Q	X	Q	Q	X	Q
J	Q	Q	Z	Q	Z	Q	Z	Z	Q	Q	Z	Q	Z
X	Q	Q	Q	Q	X	Q	X	Q	P	Q	Q	Q	Q
X	X	X	X	Q	Q	Q	X	Q	Q	X	Q	X	T
X	O	Q	Q	X	Q	X	Q	X	Q	X	Q	X	Q
X	Q	Q	Q	X	X	E	Q	X	Q	X	X	Q	Q
X	X	X	N	X	X	Q	X	Q	X	Q	Q	S	Q
Q	X	Q	X	X	X	X	B	Q	X	Q	X	X	X
Q	X	H	Q	Q	Q	X	X	X	Q	X	Q	X	X
X	Q	X	Q	X	X	Q	X	Q	X	T	X	Q	X
X	X	X	X	X	X	Q	Q	Q	Q	Q	I	Q	Q
X	Q	Q	Q	X	H	X	Q	A	Q	X	Q	Q	X
Q	Q	Q	X	X	X	Q	Q	Q	X	X	X	Q	X

Jesus

Memory Verse

Jesus said, "Let the little children come to Me."
Matthew 19:14 (NIV)

For the Teacher

Duplicate the patterns on pages 44 and 45 onto cardboard. Place the heart pattern on a folded piece of paper with the broken lines on the fold. Cut the heart, unfold, then trace onto cardboard. Make one pattern for every few children to share. Provide white and colorful poster board, yarn, crayons or markers, fabric scraps, cotton balls, a hole punch, brass paper fasteners, scissors, and glue. After punching holes for the children, show them how to tie a 30-inch yarn length to one hole in the swing, thread it up through the child's hand, and tie it to one hole in the rainbow or heart. Do the same beginning with the other hole in the swing.

Introduction

Jesus loves children. One day people brought their children to see Jesus. His friends tried to stop them. Maybe they thought Jesus was too busy for children. But Jesus wanted the children to come to Him. Jesus prayed for the children. The children loved Jesus. Jesus listens when children talk to Him. Jesus wants adults to love Jesus just like children love Him.

Jesus Loves Me Room Sign

Trace the children and rainbow or heart patterns onto poster board. Print *Jesus loves (your name)* on the heart or rainbow. Color it and glue cotton balls on the rainbow for clouds. Draw features on the child. Add yarn hair and fabric clothes. Your teacher will punch holes in the rainbow or heart, the swing seat, and the child's body, legs, and hands. Watch as your teacher threads yarn through the holes. Tie the two yarn pieces together at the top. Attach legs with paper fasteners.

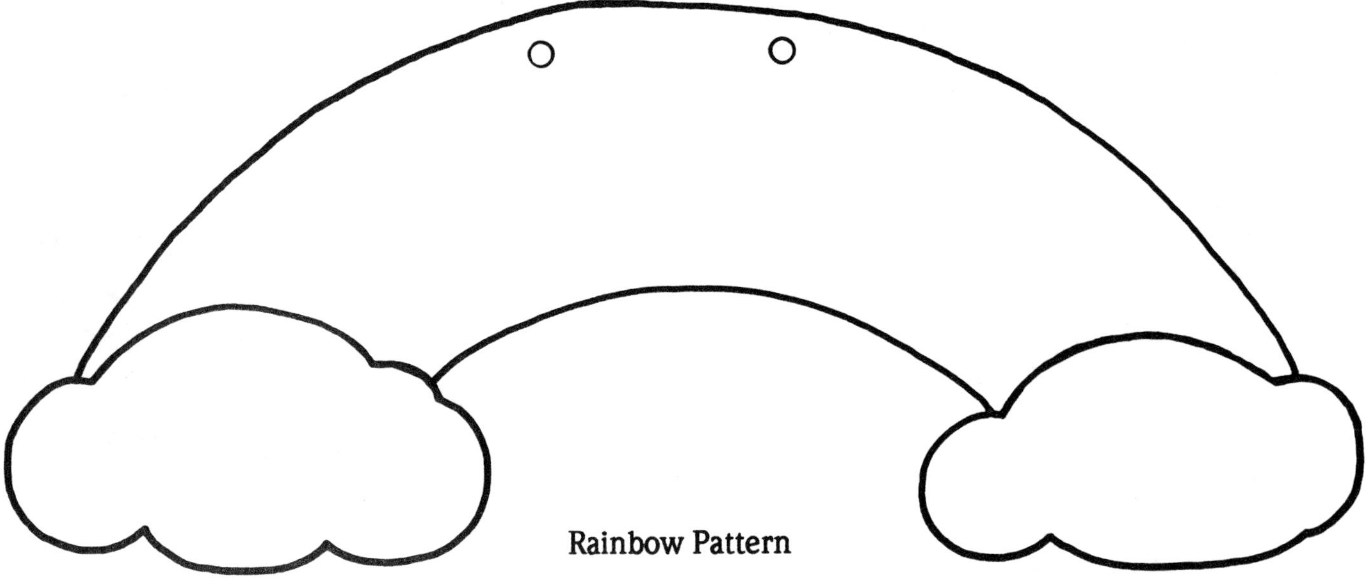

Rainbow Pattern

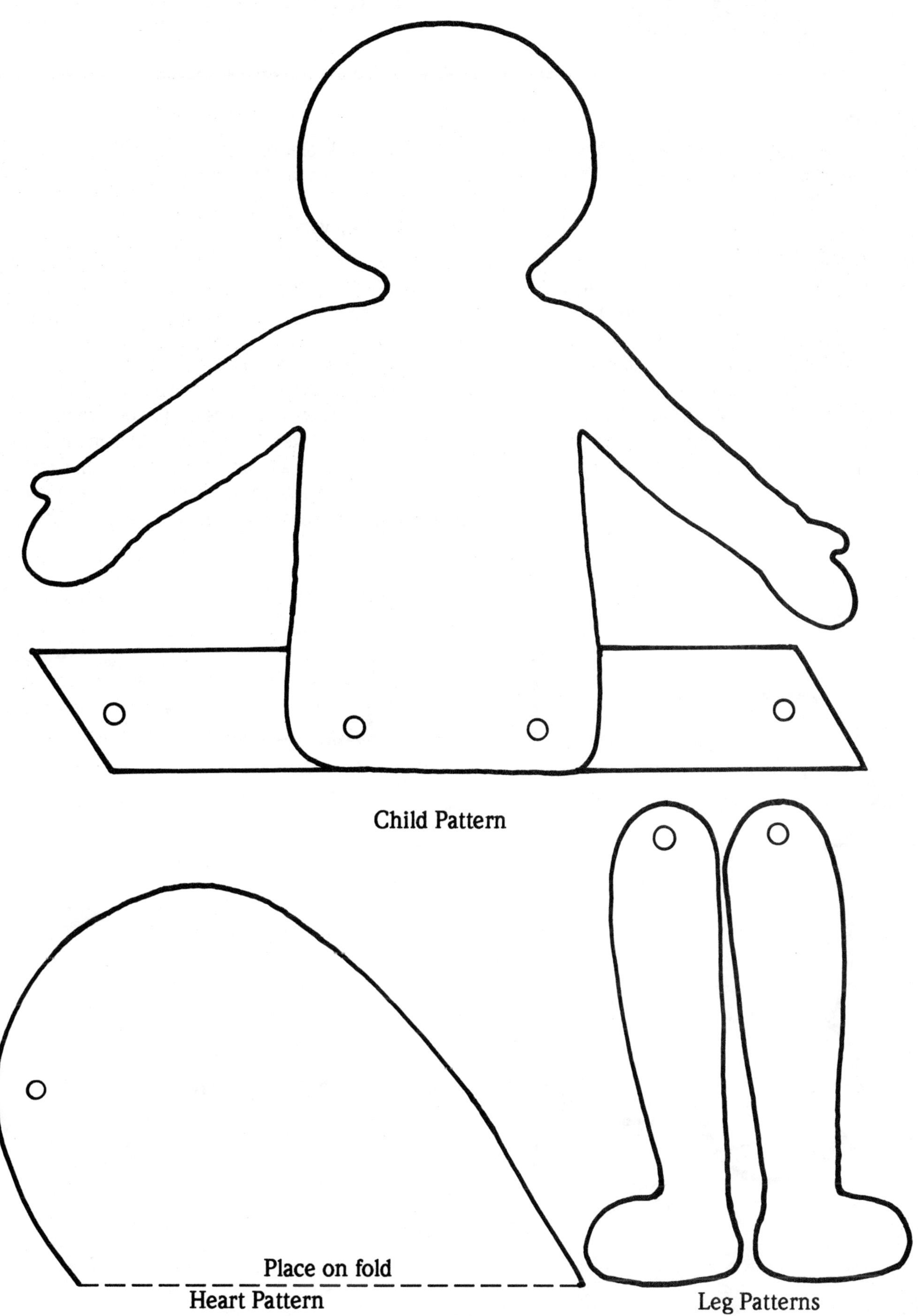

Child Pattern
Place on fold
Heart Pattern
Leg Patterns

Memory Verse

Whoever wants to become great among you must be your servant.
Matthew 20:26 (NIV)

For the Teacher

Duplicate ten bear patterns for each child from construction paper or wrapping paper. For each child, cut the center from a pizza cardboard or use an 11-inch dinner plate to make a cardboard circle and a 6-inch saucer to draw a hole in the center. Cut out the center hole to form a wreath. Give each child a 15-inch length of ribbon.

Introduction

A mother asked Jesus for a special favor for her two sons, James and John. She wanted Jesus to choose them as His very best friends in heaven. She wished they could be more important than the others. Jesus' other friends were very angry with James and John. Jesus said good friends must be kind and serve each other. Jesus loves everyone just the same. No person is more important than another. Jesus asks each person to serve others.

Bear with One Another Wreath

Decorate the bears with markers or crayons. Print the names of family members or friends on several bears. On one bear, print the words, *Bear With One Another.* Cut out the bears and glue them to the wreath. Tie a ribbon bow and staple to the wreath. Cover the staple with tape to prevent scratching. Hang the wreath in your room as a reminder to pray for each person. Thank God for your friends and family.

Memory Verse

You may ask Me for anything in My Name, and I will do it.
John 14:14 (NIV)

For the Teacher

Duplicate this page for each child. Provide tissue paper or facial tissue, bright crepe paper, clay pots or decorated paper cups, chenille wire, glue, and scissors. Drip glue inside the cup or pot before adding tissue for added reinforcement.

Introduction

Worried his son would die, a royal official asked Jesus to heal his sick son. Jesus told him to go home, his son would be okay. On the way home the man's servants met him and said his son was well. When he asked what time the boy was healed, he discovered it was the exact time Jesus said, "Your son will live." Jesus always does what He says He will do.

Get-Well Rosy Posies

Make a gift to cheer up a friend. Cut eight petals from crepe paper for each posy. Stack four petals on top of each other and gather them in the center. Wrap chenille wire around them. Make another posy. Twist the two chenille wires together to make a full blossom. Make several blossoms with varying stem lengths. Cut out the memory verse, color it, and glue it to the paper cup or clay pot. Stand the posies in the cup or pot and stuff tissue around them to hold them in place.

> # You may ask Me for anything in My Name, and I will do it.
>
> ## — John 14:14 (NIV)

Petal Pattern

Completed Posies

Peter

Fisher of Men Invitation

Lay the fish pattern on construction paper. Trace around the outside edges of the fish. Then, tape the fish pattern to the paper. Lift the fin flaps and trace. (Do not trace along the fold.) Cut out the fish. Carefully cut the lines along the fins. Fold one fin to the left. Fold the other fin to the right. Tie yarn or string through the hole your teacher punches in the fish. Fold a piece of 12 x 18-inch poster board in half. Cut out the word box and glue it on the front of the card. Draw a fishing pole and pond on the front of the card. Your teacher will punch a hole at the end of the fishing pole. Open the card and print, *Dear (friend's name), Will you come to Sunday School with me next Sunday? Your friend, (your name).* Fold the card and thread the yarn through the hole. Tape the yarn on the back of the card. Open the card and watch the fish get reeled in.

Memory Verse

Jesus said… "I will make you…fishers of men."
Mark 1:17

For the Teacher

Duplicate pattern pages 48 and 49 for each child. Cut out each fish. Cut fins along the solid lines. Fold along the broken lines. Provide a hole punch, 12 x 18-inch poster board, construction paper, scissors, tape, yarn, crayons, and markers. After the children cut out their construction paper fish, punch a hole in each fish near the mouth. Also, fold the card and punch a hole at the end of pole they draw.

Introduction

Jesus picked twelve men to be His helpers. One day Jesus was walking beside a lake called Galilee. He saw two fishermen, Peter and Andrew, throwing a net into the lake to catch fish. Jesus called, "Come and follow Me. I will make you fishers of men." Immediately, they followed Jesus. Peter became Jesus' friend.

Completed Card

Fishing for an Answer

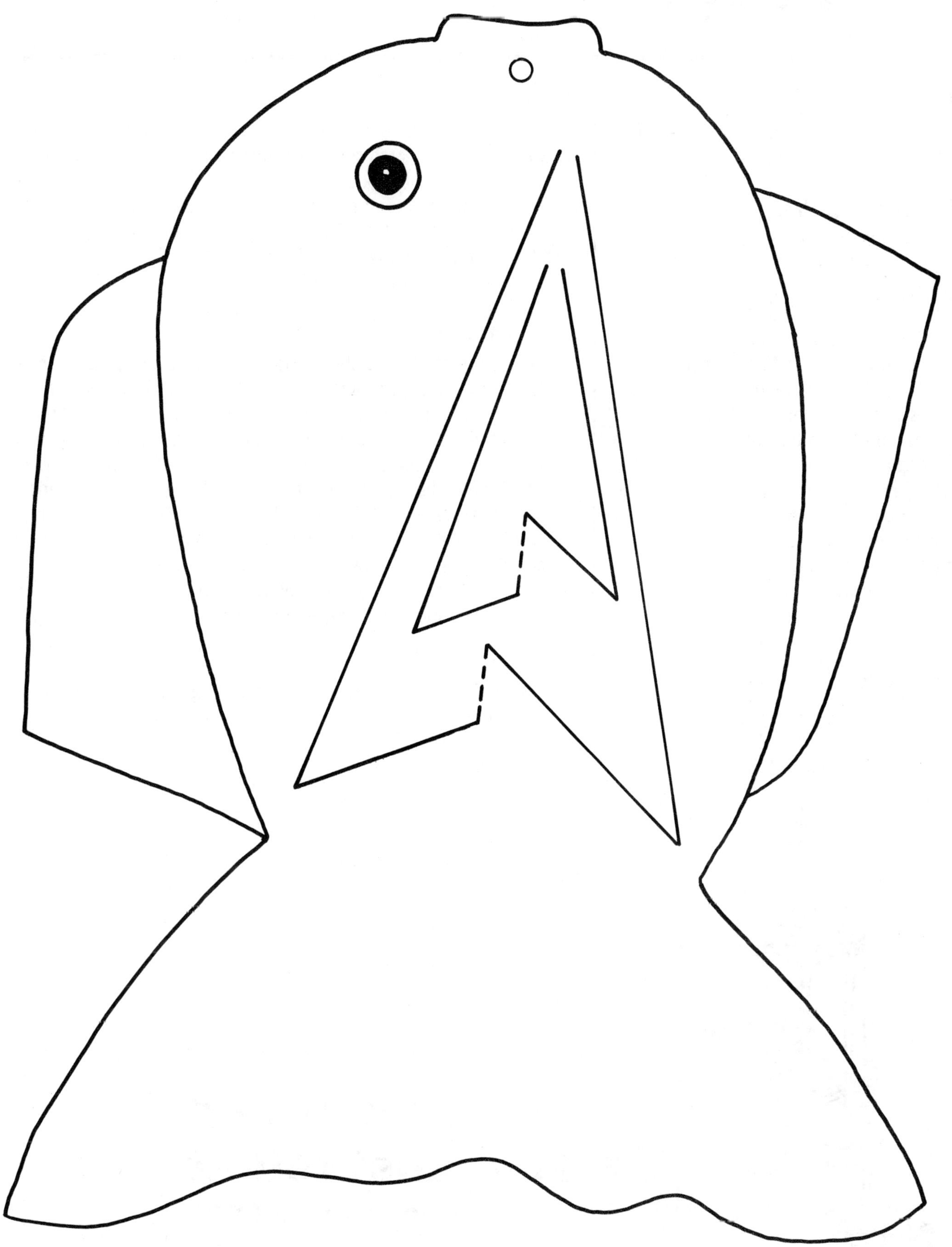

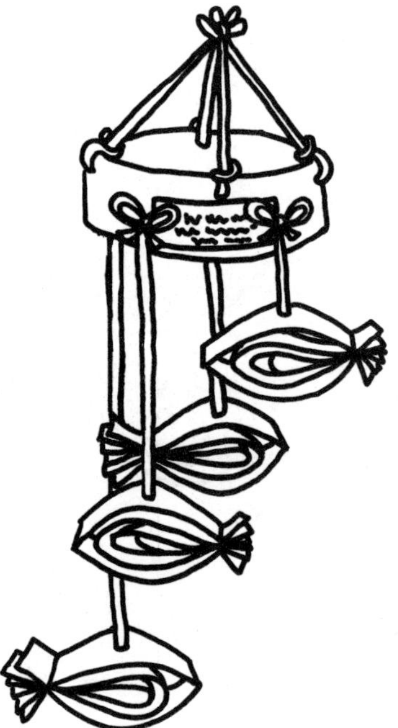

Peter

Memory Verse

Jesus answered… "You must follow Me."
John 21:22 (NIV)

For the Teacher

Duplicate this page for each child. Using three different colors of construction paper, cut the first color into 1 x 16-inch lengths. Cut the second color into 1 x 13-inch lengths. Cut the third color into 1 x 10-inch lengths. Cut yarn into 18-inch lengths, four for each child. Cut four additional yarn pieces in varying lengths, from 10 to 18 inches, for each child. Cut the bottom off a 2-liter plastic bottle and cut the bottle at 3-inch intervals to form rings. Cut one ring for each child. (The memory verse will cover any remaining label.) Punch four evenly spaced holes around the top and bottom of each ring. Provide glue, a hole punch, and scissors.

Introduction

Peter was fishing, but he was not catching any fish. Jesus called from the beach. To catch some fish, Jesus told Peter to throw his net on the other side of the boat. When Peter obeyed, he caught so many fish that the net was too heavy to haul in. While Peter hauled in the fish, Jesus cooked breakfast for him. After they ate the fish, Jesus asked, "Peter, do you love me?" Peter said, "Yes." Jesus told Peter to follow Him and to care for other people.

Fish Mobile

Bend each of the two short strips of construction paper your teacher gives you to form a loop. Place the smaller loop inside the larger loop and staple them one inch from the end. Fold the longest paper strip in half, then unfold. Place the long strip around the outside of the paper loops and staple one inch from the end. Your teacher will punch a hole in the top of the outside loop. Make four fish. String various lengths of yarn through the holes in the fish (tie one yarn piece in each fish). Tie a fish onto each hole in the bottom of the plastic ring. Tie an 18-inch length of yarn in each hole in the top of the ring. Tie the ends in a knot for a hanger. Cut out, color, and glue the memory verse on the plastic ring to cover any remaining label paper.

HINT: Paper clips opened slightly make good hangers for mobiles and pictures.

Completed Mobile

Jesus answered . . .
"You must follow Me."
— John 21:22 (NIV)

Memory Verse

Silver or gold I do not have, but what I have I give you.
Acts 3:6 (NIV)

For the Teacher

Duplicate the illustration to show the children how to loop the rubber bands. Provide 20 colorful rubber bands per child. Explain that the finished rope should be long enough to reach from their hands to the floor comfortably when held in both hands. Use in the traditional way, or tie the jump rope ends together to form a Chinese jump rope, and stretch it gently around the ankles of two people. Supervise the children carefully as they use their jump ropes.

Introduction

After Jesus died, Peter courageously told people about Jesus' power. Peter and John saw a man asking for money. The man could not walk. Peter didn't have any money. Peter decided to give the man something better. He said, "By the power of Jesus, walk." Peter lifted him up by his hand. The man jumped to his feet, began to walk, and praised God.

Jump for Joy Jump Rope

To connect the rubber bands, pull rubber band A through the center of rubber band B, then pull end of rubber band A through the loop of rubber band A (see illustration below) and pull tight. Loop the rubber bands until the jump rope is long enough to reach from your hands to the floor comfortably when held in both hands. Jump rope or tie the rope ends together and stretch it gently between the ankles of two people and jump back and forth. With a number of elastic ropes, an elaborate jumping course can be set up.

Stephen

Table Name Cards & Napkin Rings

Fold a 3 x 5-inch card in half. Fold again. Place the card pattern against the fold and cut it out. Write your name on both sides of one heart. Toss the other. Unfold the card so it is only folded once. Your teacher will punch a hole in the heart and two holes in the center of the fold on the card. Thread a piece of yarn through the heart. Pull the yarn ends through the two holes in the fold of the card. Tie the yarn in a bow. The heart will dangle through the heart cut-out window. Make a card for each person in your family.

Cover the cardboard tube rings with wrapping paper or fabric. To coordinate, decorate the napkin holder and name cards with heart stickers or hearts cut from matching paper or fabric. As you use the napkin rings and name cards, remember how Stephen helped make sure the food was shared fairly. Think of ways you can help with mealtimes at your home.

Memory Verse

They chose Stephen, a man full of faith and
of the Holy Ghost.
Acts 6:5

For the Teacher

Duplicate this page for each child. Cut a 4 ½-inch cardboard tube into thirds. Cut at least four tube sections for each child. Also provide at least four index cards per child, a hole punch, glue, scissors, and crayons or markers. (Some children may only need three cards and napkin holders, others many need five or six or more.) Cut at least four 16-inch yarn lengths for each child. After the children cut the hearts from their cards, punch a hole at the top of each heart and punch two holes on the fold in the center of each card. Bring napkins and show the children a few attractive ways to insert them in the napkin holders.

Introduction

Stephen preached about Jesus to Jews and Greeks. People who believed Jesus was God's Son asked Him to forgive their wrong actions and attitudes. These Christians gave food to women who had no husbands. The Greek Christians argued that the Greek widows were not getting their share of food. Because Stephen was wise and kind, the church leaders gave him the special job of passing out the food fairly.

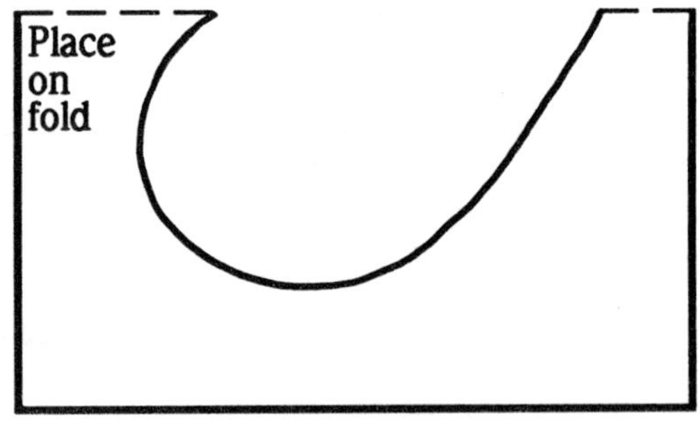

Card Pattern

Completed Card

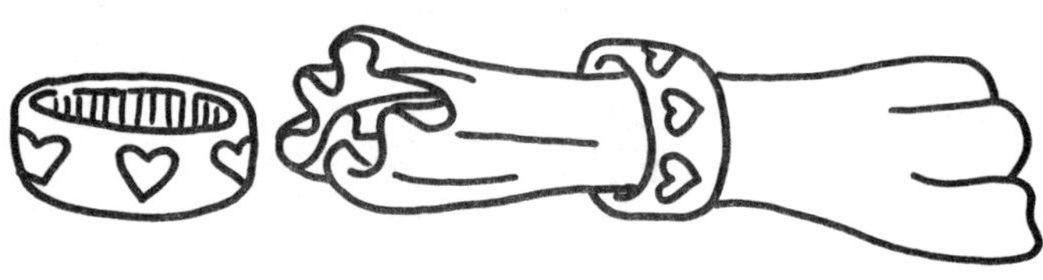

Completed Ring

Stephen

Discovering God's Wisdom
Acts 6:8-11

Memory Verse

Stephen, full of faith and power, did great wonders and miracles among the people.
Acts 6:8

For the Teacher

Duplicate the triangle templates and patchwork diagram. Cut one set of templates from cardboard for each child. Provide a 15 x 17-inch piece of cross stitch fabric or muslin, an 8-inch square of patterned fabric, a 4-inch square of fabric in a contrasting color or pattern, a 16-inch dowel rod, and a 28-inch length of yarn for each child. Also provide scissors, glue, fabric paint or colored glue, and pencils.

Introduction

God gave Stephen wisdom and power to perform miracles. There were some people who didn't like Stephen. They argued with him. Stephen showed kindness and answered their questions. Stephen's words were so wise the men could not fight the wisdom the Holy Spirit gave to Stephen. This angered the men. They secretly talked some men into telling lies about Stephen.

God Is Wise Patchwork

Trace six small triangles on the back of the 4-inch fabric square and cut them out. Do the same with the large triangles on the 8-inch fabric square. Lay out the large triangles point to point to form a star shape. Glue them one by one to the 15 x 17-inch fabric piece. Glue a smaller triangle in the center of each large triangle. Use fabric paint or colored glue to print *God Is Wise* in the center of the patchwork. Glue the top edge of the patchwork around a dowel rod. Tie yarn to the dowel ends to hang the patchwork.

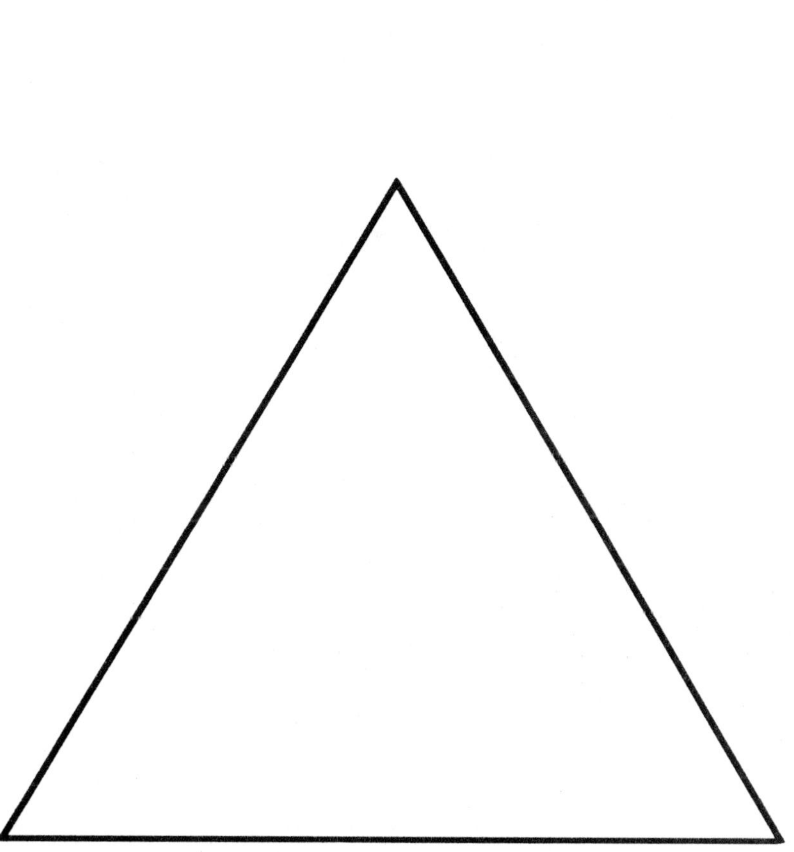

Completed Patchwork

Stephen

Telling the Truth
Acts 6:12-7:53

Memory Verse

You will know the Truth, and the Truth will set you free.
John 8:32 (NIV)

For the Teacher

Duplicate this page for each child. Provide pencils or crayons. As you show the children how to solve the puzzle say, **The Bible tells us the truth about God and the choices He wants us to make. It makes God happy when we tell the truth. Stephen told the truth even though he knew it would make some people mad.**

Introduction

The men who lied about Stephen made many people angry at Stephen! They grabbed Stephen and brought him to the temple. False witnesses said that Stephen spoke evil about God. The Jewish leaders looked at Stephen and saw that his face was like the face of an angel. They asked, "Are these charges true?" Stephen did not lie; he told the truth.

Tell the Truth Hidden Message

Begin the puzzle at the circled letter. Cross out the next two letters and circle the following letter. Continue crossing out two letters and circling the next letter (or number) until you come to the end of the spiral. Then, go back to the first circled letter and print it in the first blank at the bottom of the page. Print the next circled letter (or number) in the next blank. Continue until all the blanks are full. Read what Stephen said to the people in the temple. Stephen told the truth, even though it made the people mad.

Stephen said,

"__ __ __ __ __ __ __ __ __ __ __ __ __ __ __ __ __ __ __ __

__ __ __ • • • __ __ __ __ __ __ __ __ __ __ __ __ __ __."

__ __ __ __ __ __ : __ __ **(NIV)**

Stephen

Memory Verse

Lord, do not hold this sin against them.
Acts 7:60 (NIV)

For the Teacher

Bring a rock and a paper plate for each child. If rocks are not readily available, mold light-colored clay into rock shapes and let them harden. Provide felt; scissors; glue; paint brushes; markers; tempera paints, finger-paint, or puff paint; and paint smocks. If you prefer a high-gloss look, spray with quick-drying lacquer, acrylic floor wax, or coat with clear nail polish. Remind the children that there are better ways to deal with anger than throwing stones or being mean to others. Say, **God asks us to be kind and forgive others, even when they aren't nice to us.**

Introduction

The Jewish leaders listened as Stephen explained that their fathers and grandfathers did not obey God and were unkind to people who loved God. When Stephen said, "You are like your fathers," the leaders became so angry they yelled at Stephen. They dragged him outside and threw stones at him. As they were killing him, Stephen asked Jesus to forgive them. Then he went to be with Jesus.

Forgiveness Paperweight or Doorstop

Place a rock on a paper plate. Use paint brushes or marking pens to transform a plain stone into a forgiveness rock to remind you to be kind and forgive others. Cut a piece of felt to fit the bottom of the rock and glue it to the rock bottom. Paint the rock with tempera paint, puff paint, or finger-paint. Suggested words and phrases are shown below. As the rock dries, think of other ways people hurt each other besides throwing stones. It is dangerous to pelt another person with a rock and it can injure or kill someone. Although mean words won't kill anyone, words can hurt someone's feelings and make them sad.

HINT: Acrylic floor wax cleans up with soap and water and gives rocks a shiny look without the need for ventilation.

FORGIVE

share

ACT FRIENDLY

smile

CARE

L♥VE OTHERS

Be Kind

Trust God

help out

Completed Paperweight

Timothy

Traveling for God
Acts 16:1-10

So the churches were strengthened in the faith and grew daily in numbers.
Acts 16:5 (NIV)

For the Teacher

Cut a 12-inch fabric square for each child. Bring one cup of the following for each child: pastel mints, raisins, salted or honey-roasted peanuts, and chocolate or carob chips. Bring extras for snacking. Also provide a chenille wire and an unsharpened pencil or dowel rod for each child. Bring a few one-cup measuring cups for children to share.

Introduction

Timothy was a Christian. The people in Timothy's town had many good things to say about him. Paul came to the city where Timothy lived. He asked him to travel with him and tell people in other towns the Good News about Jesus. Timothy and Paul traveled from town to town to teach the people about obeying God. As they spoke, the people grew stronger in their faith and more and more people began joining the churches.

Hobo Stick Carry-All Snack

Follow the trail mix recipe below. Place the ingredients on the center of a fabric square. Gather the corners and wrap a chenille wire around the fabric. Twist the chenille wire around the pencil or dowel rod to create a hobo stick. Share your snack with some friends and tell them about Timothy's travels to spread God's Word.

Hobo Trail Mix

Combine one cup of each of the following:
    pastel mints
    raisins
    salted or honey-roasted peanuts
    chocolate or carob chips

Completed Carry-all

Timothy

Memory Verse

Be strong in the grace that is in Christ Jesus.
II Timothy 2:1

For the Teacher

For each child, duplicate pages 57 and 58 and cut ten varying lengths of yarn. Provide a stapler, a hole punch, tape, scissors, construction paper, yarn, and markers. Bring a 10-inch paper plate and a half plate for each child. After the children cut out hearts, punch a hole in the top of each. Also punch a hole in the top of the paper plate holder and help each child tie a piece of yarn for a hanger. Say, **One way we can show love for God is to help members of His family. Just as Timothy was a good helper, we can be good helpers, too.** Let the children share their pictures or words showing ways they can help.

Introduction

Paul could trust Timothy. Timothy was a good helper and co-worker. They traveled to many cities telling people about Jesus. They invited people to join God's family. When Paul and Timothy believed Jesus was God's Son, asked Him to forgive their sins and obeyed God, they became members of God's family. Although Timothy had a father, Paul considered Timothy to be his son, too.

Heartstring Helper

Staple the front sides of the whole and half paper plates together to form a pocket. Cover the staples with tape. Cut out the half circle and glue it on the half plate. Cut the arc and glue it on the whole plate. Color the plates with markers. Cut out the heart pattern, and trace and cut out ten construction paper hearts. Draw a picture or write on each heart one way you can help a family member. Your teacher will punch a hole in the top of each heart. Tie a heart to each end of yarn. Place the hearts in your holder. Your teacher will punch a hole in the top of the plate and help you tie a length of yarn in a loop for the hanger. Pull out one heart each day and do the helpful action shown.

Completed Heartstring Helper

GOD LOVES A CHEERFUL GIVER

I LOVE TO HELP!

Timothy

Strong in the Lord
Hebrews 13

Memory Verse

The Lord is my helper; I will not be afraid.
Hebrews 13:6 (NIV)

For the Teacher

Provide an aluminum pie plate, a large plastic craft needle, a hammer and nail, and a 14-inch and 29-inch length of ribbon or yarn for each child. To protect the tabletop or floor, place thick cardboard under the pie plate when hammering. On the bottom of each pie plate, scratch the words, *Be strong in the Lord.* Punch holes at 1-inch intervals around the outer rim of each pie plate. Punch a hole near the top of the plate for hanging. Supervise this activity carefully. Collect the hammers and nails as soon as the projects are completed.

Introduction

Paul and Timothy went to prison because they told people about Jesus. Going to prison didn't frightened Paul or Timothy enough to make them stop talking about Jesus. In spite of hard times, Timothy chose to be faithful and obey God. Timothy became the pastor of a church. To help him lead his people to be strong in God's ways, Paul wrote him two letters called I and II Timothy.

Be Strong for Christ Window Hanging

Gently tap holes with a hammer and nail to outline each letter on the pie plate your teacher gives you. Place cardboard under the plate while hammering. To make the holes larger, gently push the nail halfway through each hole. Thread the long ribbon or yarn piece through large plastic craft needles. Beginning at the bottom of the plate, weave the ribbon through the holes on the plate rim. Tie the ribbon ends in a bow. Thread the shorter ribbon through the hole at the top of the plate for hanger. Tie a knot in the ribbon. Place your hanging in a window so the light shines through it.

Completed Window Hanging

Timothy

Listening to Good Advice
I Timothy 1:2-11; 4:11-5:23; II Timothy 1:5-8; 3:14-17

Memory Verse
Set an example for the believers in speech, in life, in love, in faith and in purity.
I Timothy 4:12 (NIV)

For the Teacher
NOTE: This craft takes several days to dry (or three hours in an oven). Duplicate pages 60, 61, and 62 for each child. Cover the work area with an old shower curtain. In a large bowl mix 3 cups flour, 3 cups salt, 1 ½ cups hot water, and 1 ½ tablespoons powdered alum. Add 1 ½ teaspoons cooking oil. Give each child a rolling pin, a plastic knife, a piece of foil, scissors, water, a 12-inch length of yarn, a dinner-size waxed paper plate, and dough. Also bring a pencil and small dried flowers or weeds.

Introduction
Timothy listened to Paul's fatherly advice. Timothy studied the Bible and believed what he learned about God. Paul praised Timothy's mother and grandmother who taught Timothy about God. Even though Timothy was young, Paul encouraged Timothy to bravely teach the truth about God, to help older people and speak kindly to them, and to set a good example by his words and his actions.

Dove Weed Pocket Holder
Cut out the dove, card, and pocket patterns. Roll dough to ⅜-inch thickness. Lay dove and pocket patterns on the dough and cut with a plastic knife. Place the dove on a dinner-size waxed paper plate. Crunch a piece of aluminum foil and place it on the dove. Spread water on the back of the pocket. Press the pocket onto the dove, over the foil. Dip fingers in water and smooth dough around the pocket seams. With a pencil, push a hole in the dove's tail. Let dry for several days or place on a baking sheet and bake at 250 degrees for three hours. Insert a yarn hanger through the hole and tie. Place a few small dried flowers or weeds in the pocket. Fold the card, decorate it, print your name on the inside (or print a short message), and place it in the pocket. Give the dove holder to an older person who has taught you about God.

Completed Holder

Favorite Bible Heroes for Grades 1 & 2

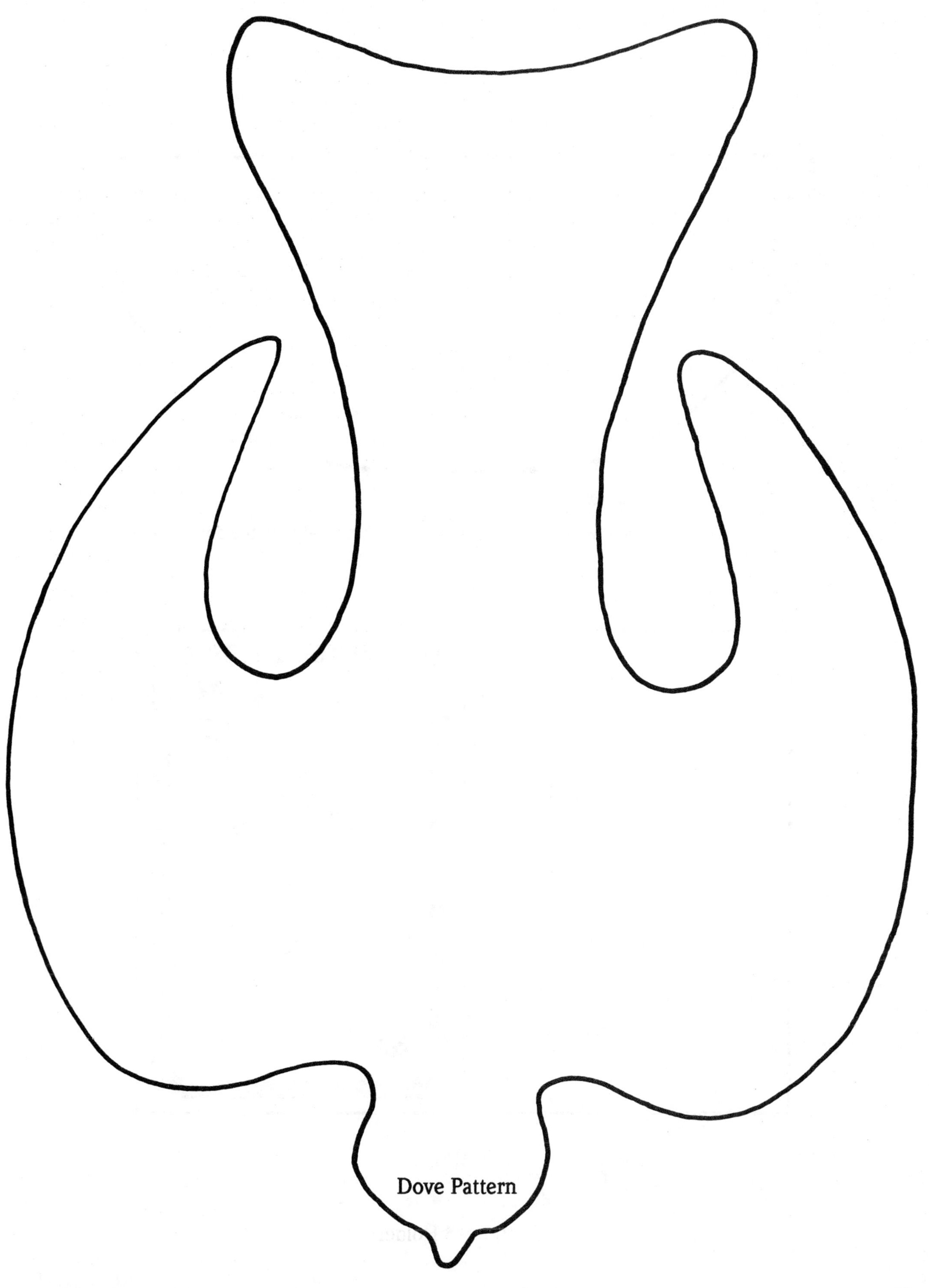

Dove Pattern

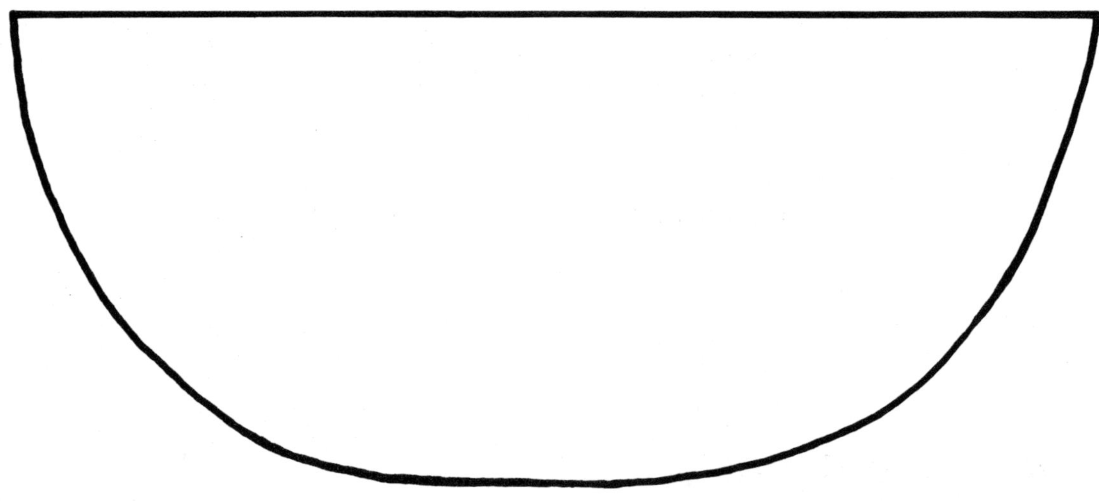

Pocket

Card

Favorite Bible Heroes for Grades 1 & 2

Answers

Elisha page 28

A prophet is one who tells God's message to the people.

Elisha page 30

Pictures should be in this order: chariot, horses, fire, coat, water, coat, dry ground.

Daniel page 39

DARIUS

John the Baptist page 43

JOHN THE BAPTIST

Stephen page 54

Stephen said, "You who have received the law...have not obeyed it." — Acts 7:53 (NIV)

More Bible Heroes —
Coloring PLUS Activities

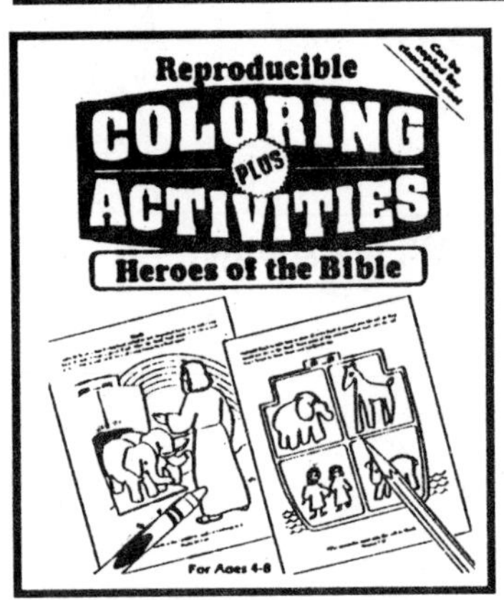

Children ages four through eight review important Bible stories and lessons and get to know additional Bible heroes with these fun-filled coloring and activity sheets.

Each coloring sheet includes a picture to color and a memory verse to reinforce lessons about Bible heroes. A related activity sheet on the other side of the page may feature a maze, dot-to-dot activity, picture to draw, hidden picture puzzle, or another hands-on Bible-teaching project.

Heroes of the Bible contains 24 coloring sheets and 24 activity sheets in these categories: Old Testament, New Testament, Bible Women, and Bible Boys and Girls. Helpful teaching tips precede each chapter with practical, easy-to-follow ideas for using the sheets to teach God's Word.

Coloring PLUS Activities: Heroes of the Bible RB37163

Favorite Bible Stories —
Teaching Activities

Old and New Testament Bible stories are creatively presented in this exciting series. Age-appropriate activities teach the Bible with cutting, coloring, pasting, puppets, puzzles, stand-up figures, crafts, mazes, and much more.

Teachers will appreciate the helpful tips provided on each activity page, the perforated pages for easy removal, and the large number of reproducible patterns included in each book.

Favorite Bible Stories Activities — Ages 2 & 3 ....RB36241
Favorite Bible Stories Activities — Ages 4 & 5 ....RB36242
Favorite Bible Stories Activities — Grades 1 & 2 ....RB36243
Favorite Bible Stories Activities — Grades 3 & 4 ....RB36244

Order from your Christian Bookstore
Rainbow Books • P. O. Box 261129 • San Diego, CA 92196